MONTANA MOMENTS

Ellen Baumler

MONTANA MOMENTS

History on the Go

MONTANA HISTORICAL SOCIETY
HELENA, MONTANA

Cover: *Bronc to Breakfast,* by Charles M. Russell (detail, 1908, watercolor), Montana Historical Society, Mackay Collection, X1952.01.06
Cover and book design by Diane Gleba Hall
Typeset in FF Scala
Printed in the United States

Copyright © 2010 by Montana Historical Society Press, 225 N. Roberts St., P.O. Box 201201, Helena, MT 59620-1201

Distributed by the Globe Pequot Press, 246 Goose Lane, Guilford, CT 06437 (800) 243-0495

12 13 14 15 16 17 18 19   10 9 8 7 6 5 4 3

Library of Congress Cataloging-in-Publication Data
Baumler, Ellen.
Montana moments : history on the go / Ellen Baumler.
    p. cm.

Summary: "Montana Moments offers historical vignettes on topics ranging from axolotls, archaeology, and epitaphs to tourism and time zones"—Provided by publisher.

ISBN 978-0-9759196-8-2

1. Montana—History. 2. Montana—Biography. I. Title.
    F731.B38 2010
    978.6—dc22

                              2010007367

For my dad, E. M. "Bud" Boddington Jr. (1922–2000),

the last cowboy of Wyandotte County, Kansas.

Ride on.

Contents

Foreword

✴ *Montana Moments* is the product of many years' research, much of it generated during preparation of National Register of Historic Places sign texts. Since 1992, I have had the pleasure of working at the Montana Historical Society as the coordinator of Montana's National Register Sign Program. Research into Montana's special places has afforded me the opportunity not only to learn about the state's history but to delve deeply into its little known facts and quirky stories. What a rich legacy Montana has!

Beginning in late 2004, I had the opportunity to work with radio station KCAP in Helena, recording short vignettes called "History Half-Notes." For the next two years, I composed and recorded twenty 90-second scripts each month. When the project ended, I had amassed nearly five hundred scripts. The idea for *Montana Moments* took seed when my regular listeners expressed disappointment at the end of the two-year run of "History Half-Notes."

Bits and pieces of National Register sign texts, the entries from *Montana Place Names* (Montana Historical Society Press, 2009), dozens of articles on myriad topics, and books I have authored on Montana ghost stories, the Montana State Prison, and other topics are all threads readers may discover in *Montana Moments*. The various sections are by no means intended to be comprehensive; rather, they include a variety of topics designed to pique the reader's interest and prove that history is not boring.

Many of the entries involve properties listed in the National Register of Historic Places. An asterisk identifies places so listed. National Historic Landmarks (NHLs) are all listed in the National Register. Towns, or portions of towns, that are NHLs include Bannack, Virginia City, Butte, Anaconda, and Fort Benton. These places are noted with an asterisk upon their first appearance in the book as the main theme of an entry.

—ELLEN BAUMLER

MONTANA MOMENTS

Creatures Great and Small

Maiasaurs

BACK in 1978, paleontologist Jack Horner was working as a preparator at Princeton University. He was on vacation, digging around for fossils in Montana as he always did in the summers. On this trip, Horner's travels took him by chance to a small rock shop in Bynum. He and his friend Bob Makela rummaged through the fossils, identifying them. The shop owner, Marion Brandvold, realized that the two knew what they were doing, so he showed them some tiny bones he and his family had found the previous spring. These little bones opened new horizons in the study of dinosaurs. They belonged to an unknown species of duck-billed dinosaur that lived in Montana 76 million years ago. The little bones were even more extraordinary because they were the bones of babies. Until the 1980s, there were almost no discoveries of baby dinosaur bones. The site was named Egg Mountain and proved to be one of the world's largest concentrations of dinosaur fossils. As Horner's excavations progressed, the site revealed nesting, evidence that the mother dinosaurs protected and nurtured their young. This revelation sent ripples worldwide. Horner, now a world-renowned paleontologist, and his friend Bob Makela named the new species *Maiasaura peeblesorum.* The Peeble family owned Egg Mountain, and *Maiasaura* means "good mother lizard." *Maiasaura* is Montana's state fossil.

Camels in Montana

✺ TRAVELERS along U.S. Highway 89 do a double-take at the astonishing sight of camels lounging inside a fence along the roadside at Fairfield. These ungainly critters belong to Al Deutsch, who maintains a herd of double-humped Bactrian camels. He rents them out for movies and sells them to circuses and zoos. Unusual as they may seem in Montana, these are not the first camels found here. *Camelops hesternus* wandered the lowlands of Montana for thousands of years. Their fossil remains are widespread. Extinct by the end of the Ice Age, they were indigenous to North America and likely traveled to Asia via a land bridge across the Bering Strait. Some ten thousand years later, camels returned, sparking legends and fueling fireside tales. Unlike that of its forgotten Ice Age ancestor, the modern camel's presence in 1860s Montana was brief. The first camels in the northwest were Bactrians used in 1861 in the Cariboo of rugged British Columbia. Then, from about 1865 to 1866, camel trains carried freight along the Mullan Road and delivered supplies to Montana mining settlements. Today, Al's adorable Bactrian camels, munching peacefully in their Fairfield pasture, give no hint of this bizarre history. These sweet, docile animals will not bear the heavy burdens their ancestors carried. Their presence along Highway 89, however, represents the latest chapter in a memorable history.

Auditor

✺ BUTTE's Berkeley Pit is as poisonous as battery acid. An entire flock of snow geese mistakenly landed on its surface in 1995 and died before they could take flight. But for one lonely, matted, mangy canine, the pit's acrid, crusted shores were home for seventeen lonely years. No one knows where the dog came from. The handful of miners working at Montana Resources, Butte's only active mining company, named him Auditor because they could never predict when he would show up. He was not a friendly dog, shunning the humans who tried to love him. Miners left him food and water, built a doghouse shanty, and fixed him a bed. He settled there at night only occasionally. Auditor's long, tangled dreadlocks made him look like a moving pile of rags. While the dreadlocks perhaps hinted at his lineage, they likely kept him warm in brutal weather. As he grew old, miners mixed baby aspirin in his food to ease arthritis. One miner once earned enough trust to clip the hair from Auditor's eyes so that he could see. Miners say that beneath his dreadlocks, he had beautiful eyes. Auditor roamed the wasteland, living where no other living thing could. How the pads of his feet could escape burning from the acid of his habitat defies explanation. In the end, Auditor died peacefully in his shanty in 2003. He was 120 years old in dog years.

Booth

MONTANA has a few famous dogs, such as the shaggy, legendary Auditor who lived a long, solitary existence around Butte's Berkeley Pit. But a lesser known story, no less poignant, is about Booth. The dog was an Irish water spaniel that belonged to top army marksman Horace Bivins, a longtime resident of the Billings area. Bivins came to Montana with the Buffalo Soldiers stationed at Fort Custer in 1887. After Bivins's retirement in 1919, he coauthored a book on the adventures of the Tenth Cavalry. In it he tells about Booth, who saw service with him in Cuba and the Philippines. Booth was born at Fort Custer, and Bivins trained him to retrieve fallen game birds in the swift-moving waters of the Little Bighorn River. Booth became famous for retrieving and carrying messages. At the start of the Spanish-American War, Booth passed testing for service with flying colors. He accompanied the men of the Tenth Cavalry to Cuba. At the Battle of Santiago, Booth guarded the remains of fallen Private William Slaughter, who was killed during the charge up San Juan Hill. He stayed with the body until comrades could recover it. The dog later went with Bivins to the Philippines and further distinguished himself, but when his master returned to the United States, the dog was not allowed back into the country for fear of contagion. Left in the company of some officers, Booth disappeared and was not seen again. Bivins never discovered what became of him.

Superfish

AMONG the strange sightings reported in the deep waters of Flathead Lake is that of a huge fish observers seem to describe as a type of sturgeon. Indians of the lake country told of sighting what they called "superfish," and the Salish and Kootenai suggest that, historically, sturgeon existed in Flathead Lake. A strong oral tradition in Kootenai songs and stories tells of the fish they called "Long Nose." There are many reported sightings of sturgeon in Flathead Lake. In 1920, commercial fishermen working on the lake discovered their nets ripped apart by something they assumed must have been a gigantic fish. In 1955, C. Leslie Griffith claimed to have caught a 181-pound, 7½-foot white sturgeon in Flathead Lake. Although some discount Griffith's story, the fish is on display at the Polson Flathead Historic Museum. If these fish do exist in Montana waters, experts believe that they are likely holdovers of Glacial Lake Missoula or from the lower Columbia drainage that came into the lake before there were any dams. Kootenai white sturgeon is an isolated population, officially listed as endangered in 1994. It takes thirty years for freshwater sturgeon to mature. The largest Kootenai River sturgeon weighed in at 200 pounds. There are eighteen white sturgeon populations, but only the Kootenai sturgeon was naturally cut off from the lower Columbia River drainage during the last glacial period ten thousand years ago; it is genetically unique. There are only thirty miles of white sturgeon habitat in Montana's

Kootenai River. Although experts say that Flathead Lake could support a limited population of sturgeon that survived from ages past, and although environmental conditions in the Upper Flathead River system are ideal for breeding, no hard proof thus far places white sturgeon in Flathead Lake.

Smoking Boomer

SOME dispute the story of Fort Benton's famous dog Shep, whose statue sits along the banks of the Missouri River. But here's a dog story to rival Fort Benton's, and there are pictures to prove its truth. The railroad town of Harlowton was a division point along the Milwaukee Road where the railroad's electrified section originated. In 1940, a big, burly dog rode into the Harlowton rail yards on a Milwaukee train. Roundhouse foreman Phil Leahy gave him a meal, and the two became fast friends. Leahy taught the dog tricks. He could stand on his head, and he wore safety glasses and carried a briar pipe in his mouth. Smoking Boomer, as he was called, could often be seen walking the depot platform with the pipe clamped securely between his powerful jaws. For nine years, Smoking Boomer greeted the Milwaukee Road's passenger train, the *Hiawatha*, entertaining travelers and posing for pictures. When he died in 1949, town citizens bought him a casket and gave the dog a proper burial. Smoking Boomer was not forgotten. In 2006, the City of Harlowton and volunteers established a recreational trail. Its northern end follows the main line of the old Milwaukee Railroad. The trail is officially named the Smoking Boomer Rail Trail. What a great way to remember Harlowton's most special canine.

Cattle Dog

AN undated clipping and portrait from the 1940s in a Bozeman newspaper tells a poignant story of man's best friend.

Old-time cattleman Ott McEwen was devastated when the cattle dog who had been at his side through blizzards and summer winds, long days and lonely nights, suddenly disappeared. The dog had been his constant companion, sharing hardships and joys. McEwen grieved for the loss of the best friend he ever had. Four years later at a Stockgrowers meeting, cattlemen had gathered in the Bozeman Hotel's* lobby. Someone noticed a shaggy old dog, limping badly, whining outside the door. The man let him in and watched curiously as the dog wandered from man to man sniffing. Finally the dog dove into the crowd and leapt upon an old geezer. Old Ott McEwen couldn't believe it. He went down on his knees and, on the floor of the lobby, threw his arms around the dog as tears ran down his cheeks. Someone said he had seen the dog weeks before way over in eastern Montana. How did the dog make his way across the mountains, and how did he know his master would be there? Many a gruff cattleman wiped away a tear, and the talk grew gentle among the men, for they understood well the special bond between a cattleman and his dog.

Axolotls

AXOLOTL is an Aztec word meaning "play in the water." It refers to a strange, prehistoric-looking salamander, six to ten inches long. Axolotls were first observed in their native habitat in the lakes around Mexico City. Axolotls are odd creatures. Salamanders normally go through four stages to maturity—egg, larva, pupa, and adult. But axolotls don't progress beyond the larval stage, and so instead of losing their bushy gills and fins along the top and bottom of their tails, they retain these characteristics when they mature. Unlike other amphibians such as frogs and toads, salamanders retain their tails throughout their lives. And because axolotls also retain their gills and fins, they look much like the prehistoric monsters in grade B movies, on a smaller scale. Axolotls live both on land and in water and have historically been found in several small lakes south of Virginia City, but they are considered rare. Mexico City and Montana are among their few known habitats. Axolotls come out to feed along the shoreline when the sun goes down. They don't like the warmth on their skin. If you're patient and lucky, you might observe them around Axolotl Lake near Virginia City.

Spokane

NOAH ARMSTRONG made a fortune in the Glendale mines southwest of Butte. He had a ranch in Madison County where he built a beautiful three-story round barn. If you drive along the highway near Twin Bridges in Madison County, you can see it off the highway. Its board-and-batten walls are painted red, and its shape is like a wedding cake, with each story smaller than the one below it. This barn is famous as the birthplace of the only Montana horse to win the Kentucky Derby. Armstrong invested some of his wealth in raising and racing thoroughbreds. In 1887, the famous racehorse Spokane was born in Armstrong's round barn. A quarter-mile track inside the barn was the colt's first training ground. Armstrong sent him to Tennessee for further training. In 1889, when Spokane was three, Armstrong entered him in the fifteenth Kentucky Derby. Spokane had run only a few undistinguished races. Bookies overlooked him at six-to-one odds, favoring the famous Proctor Knott, a proven winner who already had brought his owner seventy thousand dollars. That day at Churchill Downs, thousands witnessed the little copper-colored horse from Montana make racing history. He passed Proctor Knott at the finish line. Spokane went on to win two more big races: the American Derby at Churchill Downs and the Clark Stakes in Chicago, beating the mighty Proctor Knott both times. No other three-year-old horse has ever won all three great races. Spokane lives on in the annals of racing history.

Black Snakes

As Captain Meriwether Lewis traveled along the Missouri River through the present-day Townsend Valley, he recorded a number of snakes of different colors. Among them were rare black snakes unlike any other known in the United States. On three different days in July 1805, Lewis reported these little snakes, describing them "as black as jet itself." He examined their teeth and found them not poisonous, he counted their scales, and he noted that when pursued, the snakes fled to the water for shelter. Others have since reported these little snakes in the Townsend area. Experts think they are a kind of wandering garter snake. Twelve of the little snakes have recently been captured, studied, and released. No other significant population of all-black garter snakes has ever been reported in Montana. The Crimson Bluffs Chapter of the Lewis and Clark Trail Heritage Foundation in Townsend wants the snake to receive his due. Members are working with local citizens, officials, and the scientific community to properly identify the little fellow. He seems to make his home between Townsend and Great Falls along the Missouri River and almost nowhere else. It's time this rare black reptile be recognized as a native of the Townsend Valley. After all, he was there two hundred years ago and he's still there today.

Comanche

AFTER the Battle of the Little Bighorn in 1876, Indians took all the surviving horses except a severely injured buckskin gelding. This horse was the only living thing the U.S. Army found on the battlefield, and so the men made every effort to save his life. The horse had had a long career as the favorite mount of Captain Myles Keogh. Years before when Keogh rode him into a skirmish, an arrow struck the horse. He screamed like a Comanche warrior, earning his name, Comanche. The captain and his horse served together for more than a decade until that fateful Montana battle. Among the soldiers who found Comanche half dead on the battlefield was the company's blacksmith and farrier. He walked the injured horse fifteen miles to the waiting steamer *Far West,* which took them to Fort Lincoln. Comanche never worked again, but he often marched, riderless, with the Seventh Cavalry in parades. Comanche died at Fort Riley, Kansas, in 1891. He was twenty-nine years old. Well-known taxidermist Professor Lewis Dyche, of the University of Kansas in Lawrence, preserved Comanche at the army's request and exhibited him at the Columbian Exposition in Chicago in 1893. Comanche is still on display in the university's natural history museum at Dyche Hall.

Daly's Horses

MARCUS DALY believed the Bitterroot Valley was the ideal place to breed and train thoroughbred racehorses. His theory was that horses trained at higher altitudes had better stamina. So Daly built an indoor racetrack and hired the best veterinarians. Daly's Bitter Root Stock Farm, established in 1887, indeed produced champions. One of these was Montana, a horse with a dark personality. He was a mean, formidable giant. The horse would wait for a mouse to enter his feed bin, and when it did his massive jaws would crush it. When Montana had blood in his teeth, it was not safe to be anywhere near him. But Daly's beloved Tammany was Montana's opposite. The horse had the sweetest disposition, and despite the work he was expected to do, he was Daly's special pet. In 1893, a crowd of fifteen thousand witnessed Tammany defeat Lamplighter by four lengths in a legendary match race at New Jersey's Guttenberg track. Jockey Snapper Garrison (who rode Montana to a smash finish in the Suburban Handicap in 1892) led Tammany to such a breathtaking finish that it became known as a *Garrison finish,* a term defined in *Webster's* dictionary. The race established Tammany as the East's best thoroughbred racer in 1893 and 1894. Daly had Tammany's portrait inlaid in the floor of the lobby of his Montana Hotel in Anaconda. No one dared step on it. Tammany's Castle, built for the gentle champion, sits at the top of a graceful drive near the Daly Mansion outside Hamilton. A castle it is, too, with cork floors half-a-foot thick and heated stalls lined with velvet. Still pungent with the smell of horses and hay, Tammany's Castle has long been empty.

Military Horses

At the onset of World War I, military forces still relied on horse-drawn vehicles. The French and British forces appealed to the United States to supply them with horses trained for military work. At that time, the army operated three remount stations. These were at Fort Reno in Oklahoma, Fort Royal in Virginia, and Fort Keogh* near Miles City in Montana. Of the three, Fort Keogh was the largest. The army there trained an average of 800 horses each year from 1909 to the onset of war in Europe in 1914. The demand increased, and Fort Keogh became the largest horse ranch in the United States. In one three-month period, Fort Keogh purchased 155,000 horses. It took forty-five thousand acres of forage to sustain them. The army hired civilian wranglers who broke and trained the horses according to military rules, then shipped them worldwide. The United States entry into the war in 1917 resulted in 43,305 orders for cavalry horses. Upon Armistice in 1918, the operation ceased abruptly as the military began to motorize. More than 100,000 horses that remained at Fort Keogh were sold at auction. In 1924, the U.S. Department of Agriculture took over Fort Keogh for experimental stock-raising and the growing of forage crops. Today, the fort's horses only work cattle.

Mousers

HARRIET SANDERS, the wife of attorney Wilbur Fisk Sanders, left wonderful memoirs. One of her anecdotes is about the arrival of a Salt Lake City freighter at Virginia City with an unusual cargo. In the back of the wagon was a box full of mewing cats. At this time food was very expensive, and mice posed a serious threat to household pantries. The merchant hawked those cats, each one fetching a higher price than the last. When a prospective buyer refused to pay an exorbitant price for the last cat, the merchant told him that he had saved the very finest mouser for last, and it fetched the highest price of all—forty dollars! These feline travelers, however, were probably not the first in Montana. When the National Park Service acquired the Grant-Kohrs Ranch* in the 1970s, the historic buildings yielded up some of their secrets. It became obvious that cats had always played an important role at the ranch. Employees uncovered the crumbling skeletons of generations of little mousers in nooks and crannies where they had crept, as cats will do, in sickness or in old age. Quarra Grant, wife of ranch founder Johnny Grant, probably brought the first cats there in the early 1860s, and cats still go in and out the ancient cat holes in the oldest barn and granary.

First Heritage

Medicine Wheels

✳ MEDICINE wheels are one of Montana's earliest forms of permanent architecture. The term *medicine wheel* is a catch-all name for a site type made of small boulders placed in patterns on the ground surface. They are not always wheel shaped, although many are roughly circular. Often from three to twenty-eight arms radiate from the center point. Some medicine wheels take other shapes entirely, such as animal or human forms. Medicine wheels are found in Wyoming, Montana, Alberta, and Saskatchewan, and some of them are thought be more than five thousand years old. Their purpose is a mystery, although some wheels seem to align with celestial bodies or points of the compass, suggesting some kind of cosmological template. The Sun River Medicine Wheel near Lowry, Montana, was a spectacular example. Discovered along the edge of the river bank, it had one central twenty-one-foot ring with ten arms of different lengths radiating from it. One arm pointed north, another south, another toward Lewis and Clark Pass. Although this wheel was made only 95 to 220 years ago, it follows an ancient tradition thousands of years old. Unfortunately, the Sun River Medicine Wheel was inundated under the Lowry flood control dam in 1967.

Deer Lodge

✳ BEFORE telephone poles, roads, railroad tracks, and houses marred the view, a curious sedimentary cone nearly forty feet high dominated the Deer Lodge Valley in southwestern Montana. Within the cone, a thermal spring bubbled. On cold clear days, the steam from this mound could be seen for miles. Native peoples, explorers, trappers, and traders took notice of the odd landmark. The mound with steam mysteriously billowing from its peak looked like a huge Indian lodge with smoke from a campfire curling out the top. The Shoshones knew the cone as *It Soo Kee En Carne*. It held spiritual significance and power for the native peoples who trekked through the valley. Grasses grew thickly at the base of the mound, and saline deposits from the hot spring created a saltlick. Vast herds of white-tailed deer were always grazing at the unusual site. French trappers and traders translated *It Soo Kee En Carne* as *La Loge Du Chevreuil,* or Lodge of the White Tailed Deer, shortened to Deer Lodge. At the base of this mound in 1840, Father Pierre Jean DeSmet, who founded St. Mary's Mission* the following year, held the first Christian service in what would become Montana. Today the Warm Springs Mound* is on the property of the Montana State Hospital, where buildings now hide it from public view.

Hagan Site*

✳ ARCHAEOLOGICAL evidence near Glendive in eastern Montana reveals a lifestyle unique among Montana's native people. The site was discovered in a plowed field on the land of Glendive mayor Thomas F. Hagan. The Hagan Site, one of Montana's two dozen National Historic Landmarks, was once an ancient village of earthen lodges where early farmers cultivated tobacco and squash. Archaeologists believe that the site may have been home to the ancestors of

Montana's Crow Indians. The site is significant because it is the only place thus far where archaeologists have found evidence of agriculture. Montana's early native people followed the herds of buffalo to seasonal hunting grounds. They did not live in permanent villages, make highly decorated pottery, or practice agriculture. The earthen lodges found at the site suggest a permanent settlement. Crow people trace their roots to a land of many lakes, likely the Great Lakes, where other tribes pressured them into westward migration. Once part of the Hidatsas of the Dakotas, they were known as "the people who lived in earthen lodges." The Hidatsas made pottery and grew corn, squash, and beans. As they moved farther west, they continued these practices, building earthen lodges like the ones at the Hagan Site. The Crows split from the Hidatsas and established the village at the Hagan Site sometime between 1550 and 1675. Archaeologists have studied twenty-nine thousand artifacts and shards taken from the site. These include a bison scapula used as a hoe for planting. Modern Crows preserve the cultural traditions of their ancestors and even today grow tobacco for ceremonial use.

Helena Valley

NATIVE AMERICANS traveled through the Helena Valley. They hunted game, they quarried chert for tools and weapons near what is today Montana City, and they left their artwork in pictographs on rock faces and in caves. Local examples are on the high cliffs along the Missouri River just beyond the Gates of the Mountains. Arrow points, stone mauls used for crushing berries, and fire-cracked rocks from hearths are evidence of their industry. When prospectors discovered gold in the gulch, they found this remote wilderness a most beautiful place. Pronghorn antelope grazed by the hundreds; bunch grass waved across the valley; grizzly bears, coyotes, and wolves prowled the hillsides; and rattlesnakes by the dozens bathed upon the sun-drenched rocks. Salish and Indians from other tribes visited the gold camp, watching in silence as miners worked their destruction on the wild and pristine landscape. Legend has it that the Indians warned the first settlers not to settle there; they said that they only passed through the valley and camped temporarily on their way to other places because, they said, the valley is a place where the earth trembles. Helena's devastating earthquakes in October 1935 proved them right.

First Peoples Buffalo Jump State Park

ULM PISHKUN* south of Great Falls at Ulm is probably the largest buffalo jump in North America, stretching along a plateau between the Sun and Missouri River valleys. Rock piles used as ancient drive lines extend half a mile back from the drop of the cliff. *Pishkun* is a Blackfeet word meaning "deep blood kettle," and it's a good description. The jump's name has recently been changed to First People's Buffalo Jump to acknowledge the site's use by many tribes, not just the Blackfeet. For two thousand years, native peoples stampeded buffalo over the cliff and butchered the animals below. Every part of the animal had a purpose. Women dried much of the meat to make pemmican, a kind of energy bar. To make this energy-filled staple, they pounded the dried meat fine and mixed it with rendered fat and chokecherry and golden currant berries that grew nearby. The berries, rich in ascorbic acid, acted as a preservative. Acquisition of the horse in the 1700s eventually made buffalo jumps obsolete. From 1889 to 1905, the site was used as a quarry. Its distinctive stone was reputedly used to build Helena's First Presbyterian Church. From 1945 to 1947, the rich mixture of bone, buffalo parts, dirt, and probably artifacts from the cliff base was marketed as fertilizer. Montana State University archaeologists studied the site in the 1950s and again in the early 1990s.

Wahkpa Chu'gn*

✦ SOME thirty million bison once roamed the North American prairies, moving seasonally in herds of twenty-five to three hundred. They were the lifeblood of the native peoples who shared their vast domain. For at least eleven thousand years, the plains along the Milk River were seasonally home to native groups who gathered at this place where the rolling prairie suddenly gives way to steep river valley walls. The landscape was well suited for use as a buffalo jump, one method of communal hunting. Archaeology at Wahkpa Chu'gn illustrates how native peoples used this site for at least two thousand years. Wahkpa Chu'gn, the Assiniboine term for Milk River, was discovered at Havre in the 1950s and is under the protection of Hill County. More buffalo jumps have been found in Montana than in any other plains area, but most are very poorly preserved. Visitors to Wahkpa Chu'gn can see layer upon layer of bison bones in the stratigraphy exposed by archaeologists. The exceptional preservation of layers at Wahkpa Chu'gn provides a unique and visually stunning chronology that reveals an astonishingly long period of use. If you have never been there, you have missed one of Montana's most important heritage sites.

Smallpox

✦ IN the summer of 1837, a smallpox epidemic spread from a steamboat as it lay docked at Fort Union. Although the federal government initiated massive inoculations among the tribes of the Midwest in 1832, the effort did not reach this far north, and Montana's native people had no immunity. The disease struck the young, vigorous, and most able-bodied family members so quickly that before one person could be properly laid to rest, another family member died. In the end, the epidemic claimed at least ten thousand victims. The Crows tell a story about two young warriors who returned from a war expedition to find smallpox decimating their village. One warrior discovered his sweetheart among the dying, and both grieved over the loss of many family members. Realizing that nothing could alter these events, the two young men dressed in their finest clothing. Riding double on a snow white horse and singing their death songs, the two young warriors drove the blindfolded horse over a cliff at what is today the east end of the Yellowstone County Fairgrounds at Billings. Although time has reduced the height of the cliff, the spot where they landed is remembered even today as The Place Where the White Horse Went Down.

Snake Butte

SNAKE BUTTE is a sacred site on the Fort Belknap Indian Reservation. Artifacts and petroglyphs dating from thousands of years ago reveal its importance to early Montanans. The Gros Ventres have a legend about the butte. They tell of a family camped nearby whose little daughter died. The parents prepared the body according to custom and placed it atop the butte. They returned to mourn her several times, but the third time they found the tiny form, wrapped in a blanket, missing. A wide trail, like that of a huge snake, led from the grave to a crevice cut deep into the side of the butte. The parents hurried to camp and told what had happened. A medicine woman offered to go to the butte and remain all night to discover the meaning of this mystery. The next morning, the medicine woman reported to the family that a huge snake had indeed carried the little body deep into the crevice where it could never be recovered. The evil snake that lived in the crevice took the little body as a warning to others to stay away. And so Snake Butte became a sacred place. In 1936, many of Snake Butte's cultural resources were lost when it was quarried for the construction of the Fort Peck Dam. Fortunately, traditional stories and legends preserve in words the rich landscape once so important to Montana's native people.

Hellgate Canyon

THE Clark Fork River winds erratically through Hellgate Canyon, stretching some fifty miles in western Montana. Present-day Missoula landmarks Mount Jumbo and Mount Sentinel flank the mouth of the canyon before it widens into benchlands and bottomlands. Hell's Gate, the portal into the canyon, received the name because early explorers came across human bones scattered within the canyon's walls, evidence that it was a place of deadly conflict in prehistoric and early historic times. Hellgate Canyon was an important corridor along the Salish Road to the Buffalo, which led to seasonal hunting grounds across the Continental Divide. Enemy Blackfeet contested access to the plains, and the narrow passage into the canyon was a favorite place of ambush. In 1812, explorer David Thompson sketched an extraordinary map of the valley, naming it *Ne-missoola-takoo,* later shortened to Missoula, incorporating the Salish word for "chilly waters." In 1860, John Mullan's military road linking Fort Benton to Walla Walla cut through Hellgate Canyon. C. P. Higgins and Frank Worden established a trading post that grew to a small settlement named Hellgate, the first seat of Missoula County.

Ancient Art

HELLGATE CANYON has a series of spectacular pictographs that have been known by whites since the Montana gold rush in the 1860s. Archaeologists say that they are of great age, about five thousand years old. Unlike some pictographs, the Hellgate panels contain no animals or hunters. Rather, dots, lines, arrows, and headless and armless figures that seem to be levitating sprawl across the great limestone cliff. Forty handprints in red-smeared paint, some the size of a child's and others obviously strong like a warrior's, are poignant traces of a long ago presence. The paintings are so ancient that any interpretation is pure conjecture. There are many theories. Baptiste Mathias, a Kootenai Indian, suggests that spirits dwelled in the canyon. Youths would come to the site to make vision quests, add their names in pictograph form, and note in dots or lines how many days they spent in the canyon. Some archaeologists suggest that the dots, lines, and limbless figures reflect shamans' ritualistic trances and that the distorted pictographic images are evidence of an altered state, believed to be the portal to the supernatural. Whatever the interpretation of this ancient art, it is awe inspiring to think that its creators walked the earth thousands of years ago.

Custer's Heart

So much has been written about the Battle of the Little Bighorn that it is nearly impossible to present new information. But here is a curious tidbit from the *Helena Herald* of 1890 noting a legend told by the Sioux Indians. As the only human survivors of the deadly encounter, the *Herald* noted, the Sioux alone can tell the true history of the infamous event. The Sioux claim that on the hill where Custer fell, a peculiar plant now grows. This plant had never been seen there before the battle and it is not known to grow anywhere else. It is a very odd plant with broad, flat leaves that curve like a sword. Its edges are sharp as a saber and will slice through the skin like a razor blade. Those who unknowingly pick this plant drop it right away as its leaves are strangely cold and clammy. The plant bears a beautiful golden blossom that is shaped exactly like a heart. In the center of the flower there is one small spot of brilliant red, like a drop of blood. The Indians regard this plant with awe. They call it Custer's Heart and refuse to touch it. They claim that the blossom crushed in the hand leaves a blood red stain that is impossible to remove.

Lewis and Clark's Montana Travels

Lewis and Clark Bicentennial

✦ In commemoration of the bicentennial, the journeys of Lewis and Clark across Montana have been recounted so many times that the mention of their names brings on the yawns. But there are some interesting Montana parts to the story that are not so well known. When the Corps of Discovery traversed the rivers and trails of what would become Montana, they truly stood at the crossroads of the past and the present. Historians define *prehistory* as the past that has not been written down and recorded; *history* is the actual written record. Thus prehistory ends and history begins when explorers, traders, trappers, and sojourners begin to document events, explorations, and observations in written form. Lewis and Clark were the first to travel across what would become Montana and meticulously record what they saw. Their journals, observations, maps, samples, and specimens closed a long chapter of prehistory in Montana. Because of what they took back East with them, others soon followed. The Montana journey of Lewis and Clark was a pivotal event. In a very real sense, the Corps of Discovery marks the beginning of the end of the Native American lifeway and the opening of the West to exploration and settlement. The corps came to what was the homeland of countless generations of people. The features and places they named in English already had names.

The bicentennial offered rare opportunities to discover, or rediscover, Montana's roots and to explore the heart that lies at the center of its modern-day pulse.

Lewis and Clark Sites

AMONG the many important Lewis and Clark sites in Montana are seven places so pivotal to their journey that the U.S. Secretary of the Interior has designated them National Historic Landmarks (NHLs). There are a total of twenty-six NHLs in Montana, which include buildings, districts, sites, and structures. The National Park Service administers the program to aid in the preservation of significant historic places, increase public awareness, and further public education. As a group, the seven Lewis and Clark places underscore the extensive travels in Montana where the corps spent more time exploring than in any other place. The first three Lewis and Clark NHLs are the Great Falls Portage* in the Great Falls vicinity; the Three Forks of the Missouri,* which includes the 560-acre Missouri Headwaters State Park; and Travelers' Rest State Park* near Lolo. The fourth is the Lolo Trail NHL,* which partly follows U.S. Highway 12 from Travelers' Rest to Lolo Pass. Fifth is Camp Disappointment,* about twelve miles northeast of Browning on the Blackfeet Reservation. Lemhi Pass* on the Montana-Idaho border is sixth, and finally, Pompey's Pillar,* thirty miles east of Billings, is the seventh. These are certainly not Montana's only important Lewis and Clark sites, but they are the sites with national landmark status.

The Great Falls Portage*

THE entire two-month journey from the Mandan villages where the corps wintered was easy compared to the portage around the Great Falls of the Missouri. From fifteen miles away,

Captain Meriwether Lewis, traveling overland with a small advance party on June 13, 1805, saw telltale spray and soon heard "a roaring too tremendious to be mistaken." Approaching the sound, Lewis saw "spray arise above the plain like a collumn of smoke." Humbled by the magnificence of the falls, Lewis felt his written description impossibly inadequate. The grueling eighteen-mile portage around the natural wonder, however, was a month-long ordeal with many days spent in preparation and eleven days in transit. Grizzly bears, rattlesnakes, and "muskquetoes" kept the men vigilant while, scorched by the summer sun, they dragged crude wagons filled with supplies across gullies and around ravines. Today, the great rock cliffs over which the water tumbled lie exposed, the falls long since harnessed for hydroelectric power. Although the town of Great Falls has grown up around the area and the portage itself is not discernible, the visitor can still locate the route, identified through documentary and cartographic research. Sites include several camp-sites, the sulfur spring that saved a critically ill Sacagawea, and Giant Springs. The portage, a National Historic Landmark, is under varied ownership and ranges from highly developed to near pristine.

Giant Springs

Of the five Great Falls of the Missouri, four have long been harnessed for hydroelectric power and only Crooked Falls remains. But one other nearby natural wonder is unspoiled by time and human interference. Lewis and Clark recorded the springs that make up some of the world's largest freshwater gushers. Giant Springs is part of the Great Falls Portage* National Historic Land-mark. The surrounding landscape of today's Giant Springs State Park was where Captain Meriwether Lewis first discovered the yellow-breasted western meadowlark, which became Montana's state bird. The springs bubble forth as cold and pristine today as they did in 1805 when Captain William Clark first came upon them. One large spring spills out into the middle of the muddy Missouri. Carbon dating of organic material in the water, according to some experts, suggests that it has been underground for three thousand years before emerging again to the light. Others more cautiously say the water takes a century to filter through underground fissures six hundred feet deep before surfacing. The springs daily pump out 156 million gallons—give or take a few. That is why they're called GIANT Springs.

Mysterious Sounds

As the Lewis and Clark Expedition prepared for the grueling portage around the Great Falls of the Missouri, Captain Meriwether Lewis recorded a phenomenon in his journal. His men had often remarked that they heard a sound like the discharge of heavy artillery deep within the Rocky Mountains. Lewis had been sure that the noise was thunder. But on July 4, 1805, he heard this odd noise himself. Captain William Clark heard it too. The sky was perfectly clear and there were no thunderstorms to explain the noise. The great booming has never been explained although there has been conjecture. Similar sounds have been recorded all over the world. The sounds have different names. In the Netherlands and Belgium they are called *mistpoeffers,* in the Philippines *retumbos,* and in other places *fog guns.* In the United States, they have been recorded in Florida, New York, New Hampshire, Connecticut, Georgia, near the coasts, and beside lakes, but also away from water. Explanations for the explosive booms include bubbles of natural gas released in deep water, earthquakes, or subterranean gases moving boulders. Historian Joseph Musselman speculates that we don't hear the sounds today because of noise pollution, but their source continues to baffle scientists.

Three Forks of the Missouri*

LEWIS and Clark put the Three Forks area on the map, naming the Gallatin, Jefferson, and Madison rivers. But the Crow and the Salish already had names for these waterways, and the headwaters area was also well known to generations of Blackfeet, Salish, Nez Perce, Shoshone, and other tribes. An ancient quarry site nearby provided stone for making early tools, and scatters of Pacific shells and obsidian indicate far-flung prehistoric trade. It was at the forks five years before the expedition that a Hidatsa raiding party took Sacagawea prisoner. Soon after the expedition, corps members John Colter and John Potts returned to the headwaters to trap. A band of Blackfeet attacked them, killing Potts and challenging Colter to the legendary five-mile run that began at the headwaters. In 1810, trappers established a short-lived trading post at the forks. Grizzly bears menaced them and Blackfeet killed eight of the men; among those casualties was expedition veteran George Drouillard. The Missouri headwaters is a designated National Historic Landmark, and Headwaters State Park provides interpretation of the site. Lewis and Clark's visit there was but one tiny blip in its long and rich history.

Gates of the Mountains

ON Friday, July 19, 1805, Captain Meriwether Lewis and company paddled through the beautiful canyon that we can still travel today and marvel at the steep cliff walls, the pictographs made by people long ago, and the wildlife that we don't see elsewhere. The words Lewis wrote in his journal are more profound than any description other writers might pen. Here is what he said: "This evening we entered much the most remarkable cliffs that we have yet seen. These cliffs rise from the water's edge on either side perpendicularly to the height of about twelve hundred feet. The towering and projecting rocks in many places seem ready to tumble on us.

The river appears to have worn a passage through this immence body of solid rock for the distance of five and three quarter miles and where it makes its exit below has thrown on either side vast columns of rocks mountains high. It is deep from side to side nor is there in the first three miles of this distance a spot on which a man could rest the sole of his foot. From the singular appearance of this place I called it the Gates of the Rocky Mountains." Those of you familiar with that beautiful stretch of the river will recognize from Lewis's description that this is truly one of those few and special places that time has nearly forgotten.

Prickly Pear Valley

In mid-July 1805, the expedition explored the Townsend Valley. Captains Meriwether Lewis and William Clark decided to split up, with most men remaining in the canoes with Lewis. As they explored the five-and-three-quarter-mile stretch of the canyon and named the Gates of the Rocky Mountains, Clark and a few of the men went ahead hoping to make contact with Shoshones. They walked up Spokane Creek, following what Clark called an Indian road. They saw smoke a dozen miles up the river but made no contact with any Indians. The men camped along the Missouri River to wait for Lewis and the canoes. The men were miserable with what they called a trio of pests: gnats, mosquitoes, and cactus. Mosquitoes buzzed constantly and the men were glad to have netting to sleep under at night. Swarms of gnats also plagued them. Prickly pear cacti mercilessly stuck into their moccasins and were so abundant that the men could scarcely lie down at night. The stickers were so vicious that one night, Clark extracted seventeen inch-long spines embedded in the soles of his feet. Clark named one rambling creek for Sergeant Nathaniel Pryor. No wonder that name didn't stick. Instead, it became known as Prickly Pear Creek.

York's Islands

⁂ Lewis and Clark recorded breathtaking Montana landscapes at every turn of their journey. From Pompey's Pillar* to the grueling passes over the Continental Divide, Montana's kaleidoscope opened before them. On July 21, 1805, Captain Meriwether Lewis and most of the men paddled their eight heavily laden dugout canoes into the present-day Townsend Valley. Both Lewis and Sergeant Patrick Gass noted in their journals the stunning crimson bluffs that travelers in Broadwater County can still enjoy. As the party headed south, Captain William Clark mapped the area and later penned a name for a group of islands, calling them "Yorks 8 Islands" after his slave. Although York was Clark's man, he was a gun-carrying, full-fledged member of the expedition. He was also the first black man to travel in Montana. Troy Helmick of the Crimson Bluffs Chapter of the Lewis and Clark Trail Heritage Foundation says that Clark's cartography uncannily matches modern maps. It's a wonder how he could have drawn the landscape so very accurately just by passing through. You can view York's namesake today from York Islands Fishing Access Site off U.S. Highway 287 south of Townsend.

Beaverhead Rock

⁂ As July 1805 faded into August, Captain Meriwether Lewis, Captain William Clark, and the Corps of Discovery became concerned that they had not made contact with the Shoshones. Soon the snow would fly, and they needed the horses Sacagawea's people could provide for them. Without horses to carry the supplies thus far stored in their canoes, they could only go forward on land if they left some of their staples behind. The going had been rough, and some of the men had not fared well. Clark suffered an abscessed ankle; a fall left George Drouillard injured; Charbonneau could still scarcely walk, having not recovered from the grueling portage around the Great Falls; and a canoe had overturned, injuring Private Joseph Whitehouse. The corps had traveled nearly across the entire state of Montana without encountering another human being. Imagine the men's elation when on August 8 Sacagawea recognized the natural outcrop she said her nation called the beaver's head. It would not be long until the party encountered the Shoshones. The Beaverhead Rock near modern-day Dillon served as an important landmark not only to generations of Indians and Lewis and Clark but also to trappers and traders and, later, to the miners and settlers who came west to Montana.

Clark's Lookout*

On August 13, 1805, a few days after Sacagawea recognized the Beaverhead Rock, Captain William Clark climbed a high bluff and sighted the Beaverhead Valley through his telescope. A brook running westward at his feet told him that he had crossed the Continental Divide. On top of this rocky lookout, Clark sketched a map, recorded geographical descriptions, and took compass readings as Jefferson had charged the expedition to do. You can drive to the site located just one mile north of Dillon off old Highway 91, park right next to it, and walk the trail to the top for a spectacular view from Clark's Lookout. When you stand on Clark's Lookout, it's one of few places where you can be certain that you are standing exactly where a member of the corps stood. This particular day marked a turning point in the journey. The two captains had split, and little did Clark know that as he stood atop the lookout taking his copious notes, his co-captain had finally made contact with the Shoshones. Most residents of the area today, however, know little of this history. They know the famous lookout as Lover's Leap!

Travelers' Rest*

✹ Except for Captain William Clark's signature on Pompey's Pillar,* the Corps of Discovery left little physical evidence of their Montana journey. Travelers' Rest State Park is the only Lewis and Clark campsite in Montana documented by its physical evidence. After decades of study, Professor Bob Bergantino of Montana Tech concluded that this, not the National Historic Landmark site previously identified farther downstream, was the actual place the corps camped. They stopped at the site on their way to the Pacific in 1805 and again on their return in 1806. Archaeologists uncovered several hearths and a latrine. Excavations of the hearths revealed traces of lead used in making musket balls. At the latrine site, a vapor mercury analyzer detected significant levels of mercury, an element that does not decompose. The *Journals* mention that on their return from the Pacific, three men were ill while the corps camped at Travelers' Rest. The men took liberal doses of Dr. Rush's pills for every physical infirmity. Also known as Rush's "thunderbolts," this strong purgative contained 60 percent mercury and likely caused the men more discomfort than whatever ailed them. But their misfortune allowed archaeologists to positively identify the site. In light of this new information, the National Historic Landmark had to be redesignated in the correct place.

Madoc

✹ Thomas Jefferson charged Lewis and Clark with a multitude of tasks and hoped that they would discover the answers to a number of questions. Among other things, he hoped the Corps would find packs of llamas and traces of wooly mammoths and would solve the question of the mythical Northwest Passage. One of the questions Jefferson wished answered had to do with a legend that grew through the mists of time to become something that many people believed to be fact. According to the myth, a Welsh prince named Madoc came to North America in the year 1170 to found a colony, and his descendants were living somewhere in the wilderness of the unexplored West. Earthen mounds, artifacts that turned up in spring plowing, and the similarity of some Indian words to words in Welsh seemed to substantiate the fanciful story. Many believed that a tribe of fair skinned, blue-eyed, Welsh-speaking Indians existed somewhere in North America. Reports of such a tribe sometimes surfaced, fueling the legend. The tribe supposedly possessed Madoc's Welsh Bible—never mind that the printing press wasn't invented until the mid-1400s and there was no Welsh translation for yet another century. But reports of encounters persisted. So Jefferson charged Lewis and Clark with proving or disproving the persistent stories. Interestingly, when Lewis and Clark first met the Salish at Travelers' Rest,* the throaty, guttural Salish tongue led Lewis and Clark to speculate on the tribe's origins. Sergeant John Ordway wrote in his journal, "We think perhaps they are the welch Indians."

Lemhi Pass*

In mid-August 1805, Captain Meriwether Lewis and three of his men followed a winding Indian trail west to the Continental Divide, then the boundary between the United States and the Territory of Spain. At Lemhi Pass, Lewis saw miles of snowcapped mountains shattering his hope of an easy crossing. Then, just west of the pass, Lewis's party met some Shoshones who provided horses critical to the expedition. On August 17, Lewis rejoined Captain William Clark. Heartened by the incredible coincidence that the chief of the Shoshone band was Sacagawea's own brother, they made plans to take the entire corps back over Lemhi Pass. This pass, unnamed in the journals, had long served as a route for Indian hunters headed to the plains for buffalo. Eventually, traders and fur brigades would travel over Lemhi Pass along the route known as the Blackfoot Road.

The word *Lemhi* has nothing to do with Lewis and Clark. In 1855, on the west side of Lemhi Pass, Mormon settlers founded a colony, naming it Fort Limhi after fair-skinned King Limhi in the Book of Mormon. But Blackfeet terrorized Fort Limhi, and the settlement lasted but a short few years. Locals later corrupted the spelling of *Limhi* to *Lemhi*. Although its name dates to a later time, Lemhi Pass has been designated a National Historic Landmark because of its importance to the Corps of Discovery.

Lolo Trail*

It's hard to imagine the hardships and miserable conditions the men of the expedition endured. From Travelers' Rest,* the Indian guide they called Old Toby led the corps west along a winding, ancient Nez Perce route, following the ridge tops through the thick, tangled timberland of the Bitterroot Mountains and over Lolo Pass. On September 16, 1805, Captain William Clark wrote, "I have been wet and cold in every part as I ever was in my life [and] . . . fearfull my feet would freeze in the thin mockersons." Beyond Lolo Pass, the trail was very difficult to follow. Fallen timber impeded their progress across treacherously steep ridges. Snow and ice hid the route, and the horses slid down the steep slopes. Sick with dysentery, hungry, wet, and near freezing, the men covered about eighteen miles a day, finally reaching the trail's end and a Nez Perce village at Weippe Prairie on September 22. On the return trip from the Pacific, Sergeant Patrick Gass recorded crossing the steepest mountains he ever passed. Despite seven feet of snow, the Nez Perce guides kept to the trail, and they reached Travelers' Rest on June 30, 1806. What an incredible feat it was that the men made it across this treacherous pass and back again. U.S. Highway 12 follows parts of the Lolo Trail from Travelers' Rest to Lolo Pass in the Lolo National Forest. The trail west of the Divide to Weippe Prairie is in the Clearwater National Forest. The Nez Perce National Historical Park encompasses the Lolo Trail National Historic Landmark.

Camp Disappointment*

✦ LEWIS and Clark's return trip across Montana, too often viewed as anticlimactic, had its share of significant discoveries and adventures. Between July 22 and 26, 1806, Captain Meriwether Lewis and three men explored the Marias River to determine the northern boundary of the Louisiana Purchase. (Lewis had named it "Maria's" River after his cousin Maria Wood, but the pronunciation was later corrupted to *Ma-RYE-as*.) They hoped to find a short portage between the Marias and Saskatchewan rivers that would allow the diversion of the western Canadian fur trade to American traders. This leg of the journey was ill fated. One of the packhorses had fallen into the river, and the scientific instruments got wet. Then cloudy weather prevented Lewis from taking longitudinal measurements. At this northernmost point of the trip, Lewis named the campsite Camp Disappointment because from a high overlook he saw Cut Bank Creek curve southwest toward the Rocky Mountains. He then knew that the boundary of the United States did not extend as far as 50 degrees north latitude, as they had hoped. The men left Camp Disappointment on July 26. En route to join to rest of the expedition, they had their first and only encounter with Blackfeet, in which one young Piegan Blackfeet was killed and a second sustained a life-threatening wound. It was the only adverse encounter with native peoples during the entire trip, but the consequences of this unfortunate event spanned generations.

Pompey's Pillar*

✦ REMARKABLY, the expedition left only one obvious piece of physical evidence in Montana, an inscription dated July 25, 1806, and signed with Captain William Clark's name—etched in a sandstone pillar that rises 120 feet above the plain. The landmark's significance to Indians was obvious to Clark, who noted pictographs in his journals. "The nativs have ingraved on the face of this rock," Clark wrote, "the figures of animal &c. near which I marked my name." Clark named the landmark "Pompy's Tower" after Sacagawea's infant son, Baptiste, whom Clark had nicknamed Pomp. In later years, others also signed their names. In 1875, Smithsonian professors exploring the Yellowstone River reached the pillar, and their captain marked the occasion by carving the name of their steamship, the *Josephine,* and the date. The following year, in 1876, 450 men under Colonel John Gibbon added their names to the pillar. With time, weather, and many other visitors, Clark's signature became weatherworn and very difficult to see. In the 1920s, the pillar's private owners hired a stonemason to enhance Clark's signature. Over the past century, people have claimed to find other objects with Lewis's or Clark's signature carved into them. These include tree trunks, boulders, and cliff faces. Someone even claimed to have found a land turtle with a signature carved into its shell. But none of these claims has proved conclusive, and Pompey's Pillar remains the only place in Montana with an authenticated signature of Lewis or Clark.

Missing Pages

In a dark attic in St. Paul, Minnesota, in 1953, the heirs of a Civil War general discovered a gold mine. In an old desk long forgotten, wrapped in newspapers dated 1805, lay lost pages of the field notes of Captain William Clark. Sixty-seven pieces of paper with blobbed ink and writing between the lines evoke images of the men in buckskins writing by the light of a flickering campfire. Montana scholar Dr. Ernest S. Osgood, who taught at Helena High School early in his career during the 1920s, theorized that the papers were later given to Nicholas Biddle in Philadelphia, who had been commissioned to write the history of the expedition. Upon learning of the value of the pages, the heirs sued to recover them from the Minnesota Historical Society and the U.S. government, who claimed ownership on the grounds that the papers were part of the official records of the journey and therefore belonged to the federal government. The heirs won the suit and sold the papers, which were donated to Yale University. Dr. Osgood published them in 1964. Another discovery occurred in 1966 when a copy of Private Joseph Whitehouse's journal surfaced in a Philadelphia bookstore. There are still gaps in the journals, and missing pages could still be discovered. According to journal editor Gary Moulton, there are four hundred days of missing entries in Lewis's diary during the expedition proper. So check your attics thoroughly, and don't throw away those old family papers. You never know what you might discover.

Lewis and Clark(e) County

At the top of the stone tablet carved into the north entrance of the Lewis and Clark County Courthouse* in Helena, you'll find the name Lewis and Clarke County. It's the only county in the United States with the name of both explorers. But you'll also notice that on the tablet, Clarke is spelled with an "e" at the end. That's because our forebears often spelled their names in various ways. Captain William Clark couldn't seem to make up his mind, and so sometimes he used the final "e" and sometimes he didn't. Which spelling was the most correct became a matter of concern. In 1900, Montana Historical Society librarian Laura E. Howey settled the question, researching Clark's official records. Both as a military officer and as governor of Missouri, Clark's name has no final "e." Further, publication of Lewis and Clark's journals at the turn of the twentieth century regularized the spelling of Clark without the final "e." That meant—*oops*—the county had the wrong spelling. It took an act of the Montana legislature to allow dropping of that final "e," but the memory of the older spelling remains on the courthouse tablet.

Lewis and Clark, After the Fact

✷ ON the heels of the Lewis and Clark Centennial nationally commemorated from 1903 to 1906, Montana suddenly realized the moment had passed and the state had missed its chance for Lewis and Clark commemorations. Never mind. An after-the-fact carnival held in Helena in 1907 was so successful that another, even bigger statewide Lewis and Clark event was planned in Helena for 1908. The city hired the country's leading costumers to design a series of pageants authentically re-creating the Montana parts of the expedition. At the start of the event, the forty-five-member re-created expedition arrived with great fanfare, garbed in authentic costumes. The three-day Lewis and Clark Carnival was a huge success. Events included Independence Day celebrations and a huge parade that wound beneath an elaborate archway constructed over Sixth and Main Street. A children's patriotic march with fifteen hundred schoolchildren dressed in red, white, and blue was the first of many themed parades that passed beneath this Lewis and Clark archway. Another event featured eighty-year-old Alder Gulch discoverer Henry Edgar driving a vintage bullet-scarred stagecoach. There was a Carnival Chorus, athletic events at Haymarket Square, and revelry throughout the city. Despite the carnival's odd timing, people came from all over the state. The *Helena Independent* noted, "All class lines were erased and pauper and millionaire went up and down the streets celebrating in the same way." And that marked the end of Montana's Lewis and Clark Centennial, after the fact.

A Traveler's Respite

*Graves Hotel**

✴ In June 1907, fire swept through Harlowton's Main Street consuming twenty-four buildings, among them the town's only hotel. Prominent businessman A. C. "Chris" Graves resolved to build a new hotel, but relocated it on the bluff between the old Main Street and the depot. As other businessmen quickly followed suit, the focus of Harlowton's commercial district turned ninety degrees. The fire also prompted a city ordinance requiring fire-proof construction, and the Graves Hotel was the first building of locally quarried sandstone erected after the disaster. Stonemason August Pollman and his crew of local workmen cut the stone from the cliff beneath the new building and laid each block following the plans of architects Kent and Shanley. The three-story hotel held its grand opening on June 19, 1909. Illuminated by 150 electric lights, the newspaper reported that the hotel was dazzling with the most elaborate electrical display in that section of Montana. The Graves's forty-five rooms offered travelers, homesteaders, and visiting railroad dignitaries the most modern accommodations. Even today, the landmark hotel stands sentinel. But its period ambience has faded, and the exquisite interior oak detailing and a second-floor veranda with sweeping views of the Musselshell Valley no longer welcome visitors.

Bozeman Hotel*

✦ LEADING wagon trains to the booming gold camps of Bannack and Virginia City, miner-turned-guide John Bozeman recognized the agricultural potential of the Gallatin Valley. At his direction in 1864, William Beall and Daniel Rouse laid out a townsite. Bozeman soon became a supply center for nearby Fort Ellis and for those heading farther west. Designation of Yellowstone National Park in 1872 brought the promise of a bright future. The Northern Pacific Railroad reached Bozeman in 1883, bringing the first major building boom. A decade later, Bozeman had electric lights and streetcars. In March 1891, bitter cold and roughly frozen unpaved streets were no deterrent as a jubilant, elegantly attired crowd of five hundred gathered to celebrate the opening of Bozeman's first-class hotel. Citizens, hoping their town would become the state capital in the next year's statewide election, raised twenty thousand dollars, and an optimistic group of Boston capitalists put up one hundred thousand dollars to finance the 136-room Hotel Bozeman. Its modern amenities included steam heat, fire escapes, call bells, a formal dining room, an elevator, and a ladies' parlor. Its five-story turreted bay presided over unpaved Main Street. Although the town lost its capital bid, the fine hotel, renovated in 1974, has long reflected the town's optimism.

Sacajawea Hotel*

✦ ARRIVAL of the Chicago, Milwaukee, and St. Paul Railway between 1908 and 1910 prompted Three Forks to move one mile up the river from its original 1863 townsite. There was an immediate need of a hotel, and so the 1862 Madison House was moved on log rollers to Three Forks's new location. The old hotel was split into two parts to form the two opposite ends of the famous Sacajawea Hotel. Bozeman architect Fred Willson designed the lobby and hotel rooms to fit between the two halves in 1910. Local legend has it that construction was delayed when the contractor lost his horse teams in a poker game. Two boilers from steam locomotives, still in place today, originally provided heating. With the depot just across the street, the Sacajawea did a brisk business. In 1927, the Milwaukee Road extended its line to the Gallatin Gateway, and fewer travelers came through Three Forks. But the fine old hotel is still a favorite place to stay. Its modern bar is made of reclaimed century-old trestle wood from a bridge that spanned the Great Salt Lake. The front porch wraps comfortably around the east end in the tradition of the classic inns of the old West, where guests, then as now, sit and watch the world go by.

The Grand*

THE Northern Pacific Railroad rumbled into Big Timber in 1883, and the small frontier town fast became a business and shipping center. Construction of the Grand Hotel in 1890 well illustrates the impact of the railroad's westward expansion. Local citizens were so confident in the town's future that sheep rancher Jacob Halverson financed its twenty thousand dollar construction costs. The Grand was one of the first solid masonry buildings to replace flimsy frame structures and sod-roofed log cabins along the main street. The Grand offered guests a sixty-seat dining room and forty sleeping apartments. An overnight stay cost about two dollars, and "no house in the state furnished better returns for the money." But for sheep ranchers, miners, and residents, the Grand quickly became an essential place to socialize and conduct business. In 1908, on Friday, May 13, a spectacular fire destroyed nearly all the businesses along McLeod Street. Remarkably, the Grand Hotel remained intact. This enduring landmark, more than just a hotel to the community, continues to be a place to gather, hear news, and do business in Big Timber.

Grand Union*

✳ FORT BENTON'S beautifully restored hotel, the Grand Union, once welcomed travelers to the Gateway of the Northwest, offering travelers a luxurious refuge before they set out for less civilized destinations. Its opening in 1882 came at the end of the steamboat era when Fort Benton* was still an unchallenged hub. But the very next year, the Northern Pacific stretched across Montana, bypassing Fort Benton and ending its reign as the Chicago of the Plains. In its heyday, the Grand Union was the "Waldorf of the West." It had a saloon, a grand dining room, a saddle room for cowboys to store their gear in winter, and a secret lookout room where guards could supervise gold shipments. A separate ladies' stairway led to elegant parlors, since proper women never entered rooms adjoining saloons. Each bedroom had black walnut, marble-topped furnishings, and its own woodstove and fancy chimney. From its vantage point near the docks, the Grand Union witnessed the arrival of everything from stamp mills to grand pianos brought by steamboat and transferred to freight wagons. The regal Grand Union reflects prosperity and optimism in a town unaware of the imminent coming of the railroad and the disastrous effects on its economy.

Belton Chalet*

✳ GREAT NORTHERN RAILWAY chairman of the board Louis Hill called the rugged mountains of Glacier National Park "America's Alps." The Belton Chalet, completed in 1913, was the first of the Great Northern's sprawling hotels to serve the newly created national park. Hill drew upon the Chalet and American Rustic styles for his hotels to create harmony with the natural landscape. He costumed employees accordingly throughout Glacier Park. Waitresses in alpine dress, cowboy guides, and local Blackfeet Indians created a true theme park preceding Walt Disney. Belton Chalet, with its balconies and ornamental fretwork, is the most traditional and purely Swiss of all Glacier's hotels. Inside, natural wood timbers, taxidermy, and guest rooms outfitted with porcelain washbasins, Hudson's Bay–style blankets, and Swiss-style curtains merged the Swiss and Rustic styles. Recently restored under private ownership, the Belton Chalet is one of six original park hotels. The buildings as a group, designated a National Historic Landmark, remain unaltered as a unique example of a Swiss theme park in America's Alps.

Antelope Stage Station*

STAGE travel and wagon freighting were of tremendous importance to sparsely populated central Montana in the late 1800s. The Antelope Stage Station east of Broadview in Yellowstone County sat along a thirty-eight-mile route that carried home-steaders, travelers, mail, and supplies between the Northern Pacific station at Billings and the Milwaukee Road railhead at Lavina. It cost four dollars for a passenger to ride the rutted road from Billings to Lavina in the Montana Stage Company's Concord coach or covered sleigh, depending on the weather. Antelope Station, constructed in 1883 of hand-hewn logs, is the only remaining stop along the well-traveled route. At the station, travelers and teamsters found a change of horses, a hot meal, and conversation around the warmth of the big woodstoves. In 1908, the railroad replaced stage travel, and the station became a residence occupied until 1927. The floors and partitions have now long since been removed, but the sturdy walls spark the imagination, recalling a vital phase of Montana's colorful past.

Robber's Roost*

BECAUSE events supposedly connected to Sherriff Henry Plummer and his suspected gang occurred near the Daly

39

ranch in 1863 and 1864, mystery, legend, and mistaken identity have long been part of the history of the stage stop called Robber's Roost. Although it never served as a gathering place for the road agents and no early-day murders have been documented there, the inn is historically important as a link between the two territorial capitals—Bannack and Virginia City—and one of few surviving log stage stations of this very early territorial period. Orlin Fitzgerald Gammell, who was born in 1846 and died in 1952, helped procure the logs that built Robber's Roost. He says in his written reminiscence that ranch owner Pete Daly built the structure in the winter of 1866–1867, well after the vigilante hangings of Sheriff Henry Plummer and other suspected road agents. Robber's Roost never served as a hideout for robbers during that turbulent time, but it did later serve as an inn and stage station along the busy road between Bannack and Virginia City. So-called Robber's Roost is actually important for a different reason. It was the place where Bill Fairweather, credited as the discoverer of the vast Alder Gulch gold deposits, died in 1875. Mrs. Daly cared for him during the final stages of acute alcoholism. He died penniless at the age of thirty-nine.

Wassweiler Hot Springs*

Montana has a number of hot springs that gained popularity for recreational and therapeutic use during the nineteenth and early twentieth centuries. Ferdinand and Caroline Wassweiler operated one of the first near Ten Mile Creek just west of Helena. Their first hotel and bathhouse opened in 1865. The soothing mineral water offered local miners a relaxing day off from the dusty diggings in Last Chance Gulch. In 1869, the Wassweilers gained title to the land and two hot water springs. But short of funds in 1874, they sold their hotel and water rights to Colonel Charles Broadwater. Broadwater then ran the Wassweilers' hotel until 1889 when his grand Broadwater Hotel and Natatorium opened on the property a short distance away. All traces of his first hotel have since vanished, but Wassweiler kept eighty acres and built a second hotel on that same site in 1883. The little complex survives out on U.S. Highway 12 west of town. The hotel features seven exterior doors accessing the separate guest rooms. A stone building a few steps behind served as the bathhouse. Wooden tubs outfitted each of its four individual compartments. Local legend has it that when the famed Broadwater Hotel opened, the Wassweilers lost business. So Wassweiler converted his bathhouse to cribs and imported ladies to entertain miners. The Wassweilers' hotel and bathhouse, in its second life, operated until 1904. These are the only hot springs hotel structures left in the Helena area.

Boulder Hot Springs*

BOULDER HOT SPRINGS in Jefferson County is the last vestige of the many large-scale hot spring retreats that provided respite and recreation to early Montanans. For centuries, Native Americans enjoyed the pure hot water springs. They called this area Peace Valley and agreed to lay down their weapons when they sojourned there. Prospector James Riley chanced upon the springs in 1860, filed for water rights, and in 1864 built a crude bathhouse and tavern. After Riley died of smallpox in 1882, new owners built a more fashionable hotel that was enlarged and remodeled in 1891. It featured fifty-two rooms, with electricity, facilities for invalids, and a resident physician. By 1913, the complex had been remodeled and enlarged to its present grand appearance in the California Mission style. The opulent interior included Tiffany glass lighting, beamed ceilings, and hand-stenciled walls. Following the 1935 Helena earthquakes, the hotel sheltered nearly three hundred children from St. Joseph's Orphanage for more than a year. Today, passersby have a stunning view of its four-story bell tower. Under various names and owners, Boulder Hot Springs has catered to a widely varying clientele. It is the best example of Spanish Colonial architecture in the state.

Wolf Creek Hotel*

IN 1887, the Montana Central Railroad wound through the steep Prickly Pear Canyon. The town of Wolf Creek, named after an Indian word meaning Creek That the Wolf Jumped In, grew to serve the railroad. Englishman Charles Forman built the three-story hotel that you can see today on the west side below I-15 at Wolf Creek. Its simple, no-frills style was once a common sight across rural Montana. Ten rooms and home-cooked meals offered respite for outdoor enthusiasts, stage passengers, and railroad travelers. Forman, a butcher by trade, also operated a livery stable and meat company. He filled the small house out back with ice cut from the Missouri River to keep his larder cool. The hotel first served travelers and then sheltered workers building the Holter Dam in 1910, gas pipeline laborers in the 1930s, and highway crews who divided the town in the 1960s. Now under the shadow of the interstate, its time-layered walls have witnessed high winds and waters, fires, births, and deaths. The hotel operated until 1984. Restoration as a private home in the 1990s began a new chapter in the long life of this railroad-era landmark.

Mining Roots

*Virginia City**

✴ VIRGINIA CITY was once Montana's largest mining camp, the first commercial and transportation hub, and the territorial capital. The town boasts more surviving gold rush–era buildings than any other town in the West. The Northern Pacific Railroad bypassed Alder Gulch, and Virginia City's hopes died. Gold-dredging operations kept the town alive, but barely. In 1942 when the U.S. government declared gold mining a nonessential industry, Virginia City's few residents almost gave up. Then Charles A. and Sue Ford Bovey of Great Falls began acquiring property there in 1944. Bovey, heir to the Minneapolis-based General Mills fortune, was a newly elected state representative. He and his Montana-born wife took up a passionate crusade to save the town. Charles repaired, stabilized, and reconstructed many historic buildings. By the 1950s, Virginia City was a growing tourist attraction. In the 1960s, Bovey added a train linking Virginia City with the abandoned ghost town of Nevada City. There he placed a collection of historic buildings from across the state. The railroad, while convenient for tourists, is an ironic reminder of the historical absence of this critical link. Virginia City, designated a National Historic Landmark in 1961, became one of the first preservation efforts in the West. Charles died in 1978 and Sue in 1988; the properties began to again decay. Virginia City made the National Trust for Historic Preservation's list of America's eleven Most Endangered Historic Places in 1992, 1993, and 1994. In 1997, the Montana legislature authorized the purchase of both Nevada and Virginia cities. Today, private and state ownership exist side by side. Virginia City has approximately 150 year-round residents, including descendants of original pioneer families, out-of-state newcomers, and state workers; most are involved, directly or indirectly, in tourism.

Bannack*

WHILE others likely discovered gold in what would become Montana, brothers Granville and James Stuart and Reece Anderson made the first recorded gold strike at Gold Creek, near present-day Drummond, in 1858. The first real stampeders, however, came a few years later. John White and company discovered gold along Grasshopper Creek in 1862. Word spread across the Continental Divide, where hundreds of miners had spent a long winter. The word of gold discoveries at the Salmon, Idaho, diggings lured them there, but the placers could hardly support so many hundreds, even thousands, of miners staking claims. So with the first word of new discoveries at Grasshopper Creek, miners flooded the trail across the Continental Divide to Grasshopper Creek. Rumors flew that a man could shake gold dust out of the sagebrush since gold was so easy to find. The makeshift boomtown of Bannack grew to serve this first wild and crazy population. But there is only so much placer gold, and there are only so many claims to be staked. Idle miners hung around, waiting for word of the next discovery. It wasn't far in the future. Word leaked out about the Alder Gulch discoveries, and in early June 1863 hundreds deserted Bannack for more golden opportunities. After the creation of Montana Territory on May 26, 1864, Bannack served briefly as the territorial capital, but in 1865 the capital moved to Virginia City along with most of the population. Bannack continued to survive as a sleepy little mining town until the 1950s when it became a state park. Today, a few relics from the early period and homes and buildings of later nineteenth century construction make Bannack, a National Historic Landmark, a ghost town worth exploring.

Nevada City

GOLD discoveries at Alder Gulch on May 26, 1863, brought the first wave of miners stampeding to the area. Nine booming gold camps quickly sprawled along remote Alder Gulch. Nevada City and Virginia City were sister cities, the largest population centers that rivaled each other. In December 1863, Nevada City's main street was the scene of the famous miners' court trial and hanging of George Ives. Ives was tried and convicted for the murder of a young German immigrant, Nicholas Tbalt. At least one thousand people attended the trial. Wilbur Sanders was the young prosecutor whose courage and eloquence laid the foundation for his illustrious legal career. This event was the catalyst for the forming of the vigilantes who would hang some twenty-four men in the coming months. By 1865 dozens of stores and cabins sprawled over six blocks, but by 1876 only a few residents remained at Nevada City. The gold dredges later came through, leaving piles of tailings as big as barns, and by 1920 the highway had cut the town in half. By the 1950s, Cora and Alfred Finney were the only residents. Great Falls legislator Charles Bovey and his wife, Sue, began collecting buildings in the early 1940s. Acquiring Nevada City from Lester and Mary Stiles, they began to place buildings at the site in 1959. Nevada City became a haven for endangered structures; today, more than ninety buildings from across Montana line the streets. The State of Montana purchased the Bovey properties in 1997 and maintains the historic resources at Nevada City.

Mining Camp Courthouses

✴ THE gold rush–era towns of Bannack and Virginia City have something in common that has gone almost unnoticed. Bannack, originally the county seat of Beaverhead County, and Virginia City, the county seat of Madison County, share courthouses of very similar design built almost at the same time in the mid-1870s. Loren Olds was the architect of both buildings. While the Madison County courthouse* in Virginia City still serves the public by housing county offices and the county courtroom, Bannack's courthouse is known today as the Meade Hotel.* That's because in 1881, the seat of Beaverhead County moved to Dillon. The courthouse sat empty until 1888 when Dr. John Meade remodeled it into a hotel. If you have visited each of these two buildings, you may have noticed especially that their grand staircases are identical. These gracefully curving staircases are distinctive, with beautiful newel posts and banisters, manufactured in sections, by the same unknown competent craftsman. Each staircase has a window with a very deep sill, almost like a window seat. The two courthouses, also similar in exterior appearance, are important landmarks not only because they recall early territorial justice but also because they were among the first architect-designed buildings on the Montana frontier.

Adobetown

✴ THE peak population at Alder Gulch in present-day Madison County was at least ten thousand. The colorful mining camps were so numerous that contemporaries named it the Fourteen-mile City. Adobetown was one of the many settlements that once lined the gulch. Centrally located a mile below Nevada City, it took its name from the dwellings miners built of adobe bricks they fashioned from mud and grass. The small settlement lay in one of the richest sections of the gulch. In 1864 alone, it was a hub of activity that reportedly yielded $350,000 in gold. In its heyday, the area around Adobetown and Nevada City supported some seventy-five to one hundred placer claims, each employing five to twelve men. Salaries ranged from five to eight dollars a day. When the fortunes of rival Nevada City waned, Adobetown received its official designation as post office in 1875. Nicholas Carey, and later his wife, Mary, served as postmasters until the office closed in 1907. Adobetown once boasted a store, blacksmith shop, two hotels, and a school. The school, built in 1873, served the Careys' thirteen children and other Adobetown youngsters until 1923. Moved to Virginia City in 1960, the school today houses a quaint shop of unique collectibles.

Helena Historic District*

MONTANA's historic capital city lies tucked along a crooked path where Last Chance Creek once meandered. Along the banks in 1864, down-on-their-luck prospectors discovered a rich vein. Cabins and sluice boxes soon filled the gulch, and by 1869 the area had given up nearly 18 million dollars in gold. But the humble 1870s miners' housing at Reeder's Alley recalls that for every lucky miner, hundreds drew blanks. Fire was a constant danger. The hilltop sentinel, "Guardian of the Gulch," is Helena's symbolic protector. The Northern Pacific's arrival in 1883 helped transform the crude mining camp into a cosmopolitan city. While other gold camps dwindled into ghost towns, fortunes made in mining, cattle, and banking financed opulent West Side mansions. As the seat of government, Helena's stately courthouse* was both territorial and state capitol from 1886 to 1902, when the present Capitol replaced it. Mining fortunes financed the regal St. Helena Cathedral,* Helena's architectural centerpiece. The lofty spires harmonize with the red roofs of Carroll College to the north. But the heart of Helena's modern-day pulse is its picturesque downtown. The architectural gems of Last Chance Gulch, considered by many the most historic mile in Montana, are a testament to the millionaires and politicians who authored Montana's future.

Hog 'Em

Hog 'Em was originally the name for the town of Springville, one of the first-named towns in Montana Territory. With gold discoveries in the mid-1860s, greedy miners staked out claims over such a wide area that miners named this camp Hog 'Em. Other local camps were Beat 'Em, Cheat 'Em, Rob 'Em, and Sinch 'Em. Hog 'Em was known as the "father of the 'Ems." When the post office came to Hog 'Em, officials didn't like the name so they changed it to Springville. Springville took its name from nearby warm water springs. The tiny settlement was a stopping place for trappers, traders, and, later, freighters and stagecoaches. In 1879, the Springville post office moved to Bedford and Hog 'Em ceased to exist. Only a few foundations and a small cemetery remain. You may have heard the local myth that the cemetery contains the graves of suicides and murder victims. But the truth is that only two of its silent occupants have actually been identified. Jack Wright committed suicide in the Missouri River, date unknown, and Michael O'Keefe died in 1878 of complications from a fall down a mineshaft.

Union City*

During the latter 1860s, placer gold was mostly exhausted and lode mining was very expensive, requiring financial backing and heavy equipment. Few attempted such ventures until the railroad simplified shipping machinery to Montana, but B. F. Christenot was one man who tried. After successfully placer mining at Alder Gulch, he hid a small fortune in gold on his person. He traveled to Philadelphia to convince investors to back construction of a mill at Union City, high above Alder Gulch. Twenty-six ox-drawn wagons brought the massive equipment over the Bozeman Trail and up the tiny winding road to Union City. The mill was operating by spring 1867. Most milling of this period employed stamping, but the Union City operation used Chilean rollers to crush the quartz. Although the mill was reportedly the most efficient in the territory, the ore was soon exhausted, and the mill closed within a year. The lode produced sixty thousand dollars in gold, but the equipment alone cost eighty thousand dollars, and the operation failed. Forty men worked at the Christenot Mill at its peak, and the site, stabilized by the Bureau of Land Management and Christenot descendants, represents comprehensive gold milling technology. If you have a vehicle that will make it up the treacherous road, you can visit the ruins of this important site. On the way there, you'll see one lonely grave, a reminder of the isolation and brevity of this remote site.

Unionville

IN the months following the gold strike at Last Chance, while men worked to recover the more easily obtained gold near the discovery site, others discovered gold veins to the south where the main gulch divides into Grizzly and Oro Fino gulches. James Whitlach made the first lode discovery in the fall of 1864. Discovery of the Whitlach-Union Mine inspired others to comb the surrounding hillsides and explore the gulches. Discoveries followed, and small mining camps dotted the area, with Helena at the hub of these smaller operations. The main lode-mining settlement was Unionville, where the Whitlach-Union Mine produced 3½ million dollars between 1864 and 1872. The Spring Hill Mine was discovered in 1870 in Grizzly Gulch. The Spring Hill's major contribution lay in the twenty-three thousand tons of flux it provided between 1885 and 1890 for the territory's first silver-lead smelter at Wickes, eighteen miles south of Helena. Mining at the Whitlach-Union and the Spring Hill mines continued into the mid-twentieth century, but Whitlatch himself lost his vast fortune. Impoverished and down on his luck in 1890, he took his own life in San Francisco.

Pony*

TECUMSEH SMITH discovered gold in the mid-1860s along a creek nestled against the Tobacco Root Mountains. This prospector was a man of unusually small stature, and his fellow miners consequently called him "Pony." Smith moved on, leaving his nickname attached to the creek where he found gold. In 1875, a settlement bearing his nickname, Pony, grew to serve local miners. Pony's early population reflected the whims of the gold seekers, growing larger when a miner struck pay dirt and dwindling when someone found a bigger lode somewhere else. By the 1880s, mines like the Boss Tweed and the Clipper were yielding fortunes in gold ore. Pony was lucky when the Northern Pacific Railroad extended its tracks to the town. At the turn of the twentieth century, the mines began to play out, but cyanide processing sparked new interest in the area. Pony prospered, acquiring telephone service, electricity, and a more urban appearance. Masons and carpenters produced fine buildings and homes. Pony had a twelve thousand dollar school, a public hall, two hotels, a newspaper, a bank, and numerous other businesses. Mining again waned after 1910, and Pony's economy shifted to serve the surrounding agricultural community. Today, log and frame structures of the 1870s and substantial buildings of the early twentieth century remain to chronicle Pony's evolution and tenacity. It's a town as small but as sturdy as its little namesake.

Philipsburg

PHILIPSBURG is one of Montana's best-preserved late-nineteenth-century mining towns with a history of boom and bust. Silver was discovered there in 1864. The settlement was originally called Camp Creek. Then, in 1867, the St. Louis and Montana Company sent Philip Deideshimer to manage its mines and stamp mills. Philipsburg was named in his honor, and an area newspaper reported that it was growing at the "rate of one house per day." But two years later, the nearby Hope Mill shut down, and the exodus of miners left Philipsburg nearly deserted. A revival of silver mining from the mid-1880s to the early 1890s led to Philipsburg's greatest growth spurt. Local mining operations shipped tens of millions of dollars worth of silver bullion, ore, and slag to out-of-state markets, and the sturdy masonry buildings you see today replaced the original wooden false fronts. When the panic of 1893 curtailed silver mining, sapphire deposits helped stabilize the local economy, and the creation of Granite County with Philipsburg as county seat helped the town survive. During World War I, Philipsburg was the largest supplier of domestic manganese. Philipsburg's economy today is based on agriculture, government, logging, limited mining, and tourism. The town is a little gem with a well-preserved main street.

Belt

PENNSYLVANIA native John Castner discovered rich coal deposits along Belt Creek in 1870. Within just a few years, he and Fort Benton trader T. C. Power opened Montana's first commercial coal mine nearby. The partners sold coal to the Great Northern Railway, the Boston & Montana Consolidated Copper and Silver Mining Company smelter in Great Falls, and domestic users in central Montana. The town of Belt originated to serve the mine, attracting men from throughout the United States and Europe to work side by side underground. In 1885, Castner and his wife, Mattie, established a stage station and hotel at the settlement along the Lewistown–Great Falls Road. Mattie, a former slave, came west to Fort Benton, where she established a laundry business and met her future husband. Despite Montana laws against interracial marriage, the Castners prospered. John's mining operations proved very lucrative and Mattie owned the hotel and restaurant, which she ran efficiently. The Castners' financial success allowed Mattie to return to the South several times and reconnect with family members slavery had separated. In 1894, expansion of the mine under its new owner, the Anaconda Copper Mining Company, changed the town dramatically. Its commercial district relocated to the area adjacent to the Castners' stage station on what became known as Castner Street. By the early twentieth century, wood false-front commercial buildings and saloons lined the street. Further expansion of the mine and increasing dependence on agriculture in the early 1900s significantly changed Belt's appearance. The old false-front build-ings gave way to the stone and brick buildings that document Belt's metamorphosis from mining camp to city.

Butte*

BUTTE was born as a lively gold camp in the 1860s, with dozens of miners' shacks strewn across the hills and gulches. Its gold, however, was difficult to extract because water, required for placer mining, was scarce. As in most mining camps where resources were not readily attainable, miners got discouraged and moved on. Unlike most other Montana boomtowns, however, Butte was destined for a greater future. In the mid-1870s, experienced miners realized that Butte's potential lay in silver and copper, not in gold. A young upstart by the name of Marcus Daly helped develop Butte's immense potential for copper. New technologies, including telephones and electric lighting, created new demands for copper, and wealthy investors gambled wildly to finance mining operations. Butte quickly rose to unprecedented prominence in the world of mining. Its unique role as a huge urban industrial center essen-tially in the middle of nowhere is a history bizarre and unrivaled. Butte, the Richest Hill on Earth, became one of the toughest towns in America, the national birthplace of unionism, and a melting pot of every conceivable language and culture.

Desperadoes, Dandies, and Darned Good Men

Fritz Augustus Heinze

✳ BUTTE Copper King Fritz Augustus Heinze was dashing, aggressive, and unscrupulous. Women adored him, and he lived a fast and colorful, albeit short, life. In 1893, he formed an alliance with Copper King William A. Clark against their mutual rival Marcus Daly. After Daly's death in 1900, Standard Oil Company acquired Daly's influential Amalgamated Copper Mining Company. Heinze and Clark challenged its political and economic power. But mining fortunes made quickly could be lost just as fast. Standard Oil retaliated. Stock in Heinze's own United Copper Company was mysteriously bought and sold. This and Heinze's own financial indiscretions ruined him. At the height of his legal and financial troubles, Heinze's mining fortunes financed the handsome Metals Bank Building* at Park and Main streets. Nationally acclaimed architect Cass Gilbert designed the landmark in 1906, at the same time that he designed the Montana Club* in Helena. Architecturally similar, both were pivotal buildings, constructed with new techniques that allowed multiple stories. In 1914, Heinze died broke in New York City of cirrhosis of the liver; he was only forty-five. The Metals Bank Building is the only legacy he left in Montana.

William A. Clark

HISTORIAN Joseph Kinsey Howard said that a dollar never got away from Copper King William A. Clark except to come back stuck to another. Clark was intelligent, ambitious, and obsessed with his own vanity. Butte was his stronghold. Clark gave his miners there a magnificent park and an eight-hour workday. Clark spared no expense on his 1880s mansion* in Butte. The thirty-plus rooms had electric as well as incandescent and gas lighting, and a fifteen-hundred-gallon tank on the third floor supplied the household with running water. The home's beveled French plate-glass windows with blinds of hardwood that folded into pockets and frescoed ceilings had no equal in the West. Montana saw little of Clark after 1900, when he served an undistinguished six years in the U.S. Senate. Clark endowed a library and built a theater at the prison* in Deer Lodge—the first prison theater in the United States—to thank the warden for the use of convict labor on his ranches and in his mines. But Clark took his vast fortune elsewhere. His wealth endowed the University of Virginia's law school, the Los Angeles Philharmonic Orchestra, and the University of California's library. None of it ever came back to Montana.

Charles M. Russell

ALTHOUGH artist Charles M. Russell was born in St. Louis, he came West in 1882 and Montana claims him as a native son. He wrangled cattle for a decade, gaining a reputation as a man who could draw good pictures and tell a good story. Russell combined these two skills on canvas, painting the American West as he saw it—romantic, poignant, and changing—earning him the moniker "Word Painter." He married Nancy Cooper in 1896, and their modest white clapboard home in Great Falls dates to 1900. It has changed little since the Russells' occupancy. Russell built the log cabin studio in 1903. After its construction, he reportedly never finished a painting anywhere else. Russell died in 1926, and his home and studio form the nucleus of the Russell Museum, a renowned museum and gallery of Russell's art. The Russells' Home and Studio* is a National Historic Landmark. The Montana Historical Society in Helena has one of the best collections of Russell's art, including the renowned *When the Land Belonged to God*. This painting hung in the Montana Club* until insurance concerns prompted its purchase by the state.

Steve Reeves

STEVE REEVES, a well-known body builder of the 1950s, was a native Montanan, born in Glasgow in the mid-1920s. He became famous, winning the titles of Mr. America, Mr. World, and Mr. Universe. His parents met and married in Scobey. When he was only months old, Reeves won Healthiest Baby of Valley County, the first title in a lifetime of awards. In 1927, when he was not yet two years old, Reeves's father was killed in a threshing accident. His mother, Goldie, worked as a cook and soon took her son to live in Great Falls. When Reeves was ten, they moved to California. But the youngster spent his summers in Montana on his uncle's ranch. He served in World War II and began body building. After winning the most prestigious body-building titles, Reeves took acting lessons and landed the leading role in *Hercules*. The movie skyrocketed him to fame. Reeves went on to star in other films. Despite his Hollywood connections, Reeves never forgot his eastern Montana roots. He returned to Scobey several times to visit his father's grave and become acquainted with family friends. Reeves had a remarkable physique, and many regarded his appearance as "godlike." Although his fans believed the legendary Mr. Universe would live forever, he died at age seventy-four in 2000.

Cap Williams

SOUTH of the Ruby River Reservoir in the beautiful emerald-green ranchlands of the Ruby Valley in Madison County, there is a small cemetery that holds the grave of Captain James Williams, who came to Bannack with a wagon train from Denver in 1862. In the absence of a leader, the travelers elected Williams to lead the train, and thereafter he was known as Captain, or Cap, for short. Cap Williams witnessed the rush to Alder Gulch. During those dark, turbulent days of lawlessness, he again served as captain, this time of the vigilantes. Cap later ranched in the Ruby Valley. But in March 1887, he came to a sad end. Searchers found his body hidden in a thicket. Cap had carefully crawled in and laid out his mittens and scarf as a pillow. Lying down on this makeshift bed in the snow, he drank a bottle of laudanum, knowing that he would go to sleep and the cold winter weather would do the rest. Some speculated that he was in financial difficulty, and that Virginia City banker Henry Elling was about to foreclose on his ranch. Others said that his role as a vigilante weighed heavily upon him. Whatever the reason, he thus ended his life. He left a wife and seven children. Today, his lonely tombstone is his only legacy, a remnant of vigilante days.

Long George Francis

ONE of the most colorful characters of the High Line was an old-time cowboy who came to a hideous end. Long George Francis was well known on the rodeo circuit. He lived along the Milk River west of Havre on a small ranch. But Francis lived by the old range rules, believing unbranded stock was fair game. Times were changing, range laws were evolving, and opinions about Francis were divided. Some were outraged when the court convicted Francis of grand larceny for the theft of a bay mare. Others saw Francis as a cattle rustler and approved of his conviction. But after sentencing in 1918, Francis went into hiding. He was on the lam for two years until he finally grew tired of running. On Christmas Eve, 1920, he prepared to give himself up to serve his sentence. But first he was determined to make one last trip to visit his schoolteacher girlfriend near the Canadian border. He loaded his car with apples and gifts for her and the children and started out on the journey. It was snowing and cold. Thirty miles northwest of Havre in the middle of nowhere, he wrecked his car and broke his leg in the accident. Fashioning a splint from an apple box, he tried to crawl for help. Exhausted and in pain with little hope of rescue, Francis slit his own throat and bled to death in the snow.

Wilbur Fisk Sanders

OVER the course of more than a century, many illustrious men—and women—have served Montana as legislators. Our current lawmakers follow in some very big footsteps. One of the best known is Wilbur Fisk Sanders, whose long career as an attorney famed for his speechmaking began with a famous trial in Nevada City on a snowy December day in 1863. Sanders was the only man brave enough to prosecute George Ives, a suspected road agent accused of a brutal murder. Ives's trial, conviction, and swift hanging on Nevada City's main street served as a catalyst to the forming of the famous vigilantes a few days later. Sanders's first home in Virginia City and his second home—now the Sanders Bed and Breakfast* in Helena—are important historical sites. Throughout his long career, Sanders was always outspoken and not easily intimidated. One winter day in Helena, Episcopal bishop Daniel Tuttle and Sanders met on a steep and icy street, and at that moment Sanders slipped and fell. The Bishop looked down on the prostrate man and observed, "The wicked stand in slippery places, Mr. Sanders." Looking up, Sanders shot back, "I see they do, Bishop, but damned if I see how they can."

Bill Hynson

BILL HYNSON was a bad apple and a rough character who, in a strange manner, scripted his own death at Fort Benton in 1868. When saloon patrons who had overindulged began to report money missing from their pockets, many suspected Hynson. Locals observed Hynson keeping company with inebriated saloon patrons whose funds came up short. The local vigilance committee—that Hynson, ironically, took some credit for organizing—planned a trap to catch the perpetrator. They planted a supposedly drunken patron with heavy pockets in the local saloon. The plant pretended to pass out, and Hynson helped himself to the man's pockets. The next day, the committee informed Hynson that the criminal had been discovered. Deputy Marshall X. Beidler was in town, and the vigilantes announced that they intended to have a hanging. Hynson, unaware that he had been observed, volunteered to supply the rope and directed old-time trapper Henry Mills to dig a grave. Hynson promised Mills that in due time he would supply the corpse. Marshall Beidler, a cruel man well versed in the art of hanging, took the rope Hynson offered and placed it over his neck. Without a word, Hynson's life was quickly snuffed. The corpse that filled the waiting grave was Hynson himself. His was one of three known vigilante hangings in Fort Benton.

William T. Hornaday

IN 1886, the Smithsonian sent an expedition to Montana to collect buffalo specimens. Expedition leader William T. Hornaday was an internationally known naturalist, author, and conservationist. He was also the Smithsonian's chief taxidermist and considered the best in the United States. The expedition collected specimens from the last free-roaming herd of wild bison as they were on the brink of total extinction. Hornaday's experiences in

Montana led him to write scathingly of the buffalo's extermination and to publicize its sad plight. One of the specimens Hornaday collected at the Big Porcupine Creek camp in Garfield County is among the bison that make up the famous American Bison Group. It is one of the largest bison bulls ever recorded, and it served as the model for the buffalo on the 1901 ten-dollar bill. In 1908, Hornaday helped establish the National Bison Range in Montana. The Hornaday Buffalo Camp* on Big Porcupine Creek at Sand Springs was the expedition's final base camp. Today, it is a National Historic Landmark. Hornaday's American Bison Group, evidence of Hornaday's skill in taxidermy, is on display at the Museum of the Northern Great Plains in Fort Benton.

Frank Linderman

SIXTEEN-YEAR-OLD Frank Linderman left Chicago for the Flathead Valley wilderness in 1885. He became a friend to the Indians and viewed encroaching civilization firsthand. Linderman's passionate desire was to preserve the old West, especially Montana, in printer's ink. Linderman did it all. He was a trapper, trader, assayer, newspaperman, businessman, insurance agent, and state legislator. He was an advocate of Indian causes. Through his efforts, along with Charlie Russell and other friends, Congress created the Rocky Boy's Reservation for landless members of several Chippewa and Cree bands. Native American leaders respected Linderman's active support and through "sign talk" shared their histories, customs, and stories. From 1898 to 1905, Linderman edited the *Sheridan Chinook* in a building that Charles Bovey later rescued and placed at Nevada City. In 1917, Linderman built a cabin in Lake County where he authored many books, stories, and articles, among them the highly acclaimed biography of the Crow chief Plenty Coups. His accurate portrayals led Plenty Coups to conclude, "I am glad I have told you these things, Sign Talker. You have felt my heart, and I have felt yours." Frank Linderman is one of the treasures of the Treasure State.

John W. White

✦ KALISPELL'S historic Central School* today is home to the Northwest Montana Historical Society and serves as a community center and museum. But from 1894 to 1991, Central served students. Back in 1932 during the Great Depression, students of social science and history were studying the Civil War. The school's longtime janitor, John W. White, knew a thing or two firsthand about one of the main issues. White was born a slave in North Carolina. He was ten when the war ended and freedom changed his life. He came west where he and his wife, Helen, settled in Demersville. They moved to Kalispell with its founding in 1891. White worked at Central School for more than thirty-five years. He had no formal schooling, but he was a self-taught scholar and an avid reader, and he believed in education. He began his long workday at four A.M., and at the end of every day, when the halls were quiet, he would take up his place by the furnace with a book in his hand and do some serious reading. White, beloved by generations of Central children, saved his money to send four of his own children to college. On one special day in May 1932, as White neared the end of his long life, he set aside his mops and brooms to tell the children about his own personal experiences. White's lectures on slavery that day had the children riveted to their seats. He passed away two years later, in 1934, but he left Central students with a perspective they did not forget.

Julian Anderson

✦ JULIAN ANDERSON was a beloved and special individual who gave many years of service to the far-famed Montana Club* in Helena. There is no record of his birth in Hamburg, Germany. His parents moved there as household slaves of a Caroline County, Virginia, family. The family had fled the South at the beginning of the Civil War. Julian observed his birthday on September 23, since his mother told him that he was born at "fodder-pulling time." After the Civil War, when Julian was six or seven, the Andersons returned to the United States. They moved west to Denver. Julian struck out on his own, learned the trades of baker and confectioner in Laramie, Wyoming, and came to Helena in 1887. He worked at the Merchant's Hotel and then as night clerk at the brand-new Broadwater Hotel. In 1893, he began as bartender at the Montana Club. Julian was famous as the master of mixes. Even though he was a highly skilled drink master, he never took a drink himself. He served such world-famous figures as Prince Albert of Belgium, Prince Olaf of Norway, Mark Twain, Otis Skinner, William Jennings Bryan, artist Charlie Russell, and all the Copper Kings. He even heard Teddy Roosevelt say "dee-lighted" in person. He hardly missed pouring a drink when the club burned down, despite the fact that his own son Harry caused the tragedy. In 1938, members celebrated Julian's forty-fifth anniversary with the club, signing a tribute to him that read: "To Julian Anderson who never forgets us, is always constant, pleasant and competent. In sincere appreciation of his forty-five years with the Montana Club." Julian retired in 1953 after sixty years of serving club patrons. He died in 1961 at 102.

Thomas Francis Meagher

THE bronze statue of the flamboyant General Thomas Francis Meagher astride his magnificent steed has stood its ground on the Capitol lawn since 1905. The general served as Montana's first territorial secretary, appointed in 1865, and twice as acting governor during Montana's turbulent beginnings. His mysterious death occurred on a dark night in 1867 when he disappeared from the steamship *G. A. Thompson* as it lay docked at Fort Benton. What actually happened is still unknown. General Meagher was a fiery revolutionary during the Irish insurrection against British rule in the 1850s. He was captured and sentenced to be hanged, drawn, and quartered, but his gift for oratory won him a sentence reduced to exile in Australian Tasmania. There he managed to escape to the United States. General Meagher later led the hard-charging Irish Brigade of the Union Army. Prominent Montana statesman Martin Maginnis served with Meagher during the Civil War and suggested a monument to him. Contributions came from Irish across the state, and Meagher's former New York regiment contributed five hundred dollars. Irish-born sculptor Charles J. Mulligan of Chicago designed the statue at a cost of twenty thousand dollars. The legendary figure astride his horse adds a wonderful grandeur to the lawn of our state Capitol.

Baron O'Keefe

A CANYON twelve miles west of Missoula bears the name of a colorful character time has forgotten. He helped build the Mullan Road and planted an orchard in Missoula County. Cornelius O'Keefe introduced the first farming equipment in Montana— thresher, reaper, and mower—and made a small fortune freighting his crops to local mining camps. Perhaps because he came from Ireland, his best crop was potatoes, which he sold by the wagon-load to the potato-starved residents of Bannack and Virginia City. O'Keefe once had a lawsuit brought against him, the very first in Montana. When O'Keefe told Judge Henry Brooks he planned to represent himself, the judge took out a deck of cards and shuffled them. "These are my credentials," said the judge. "What are yours?" he asked O'Keefe. O'Keefe answered, "These are my credentials," and punched the judge right between the eyes. The judge didn't argue. O'Keefe was always known as Baron O'Keefe. Elected twice to the territorial legislature, he acquired the title when he had to sign the official roster. Instead of noting his occupation as "farmer," this picturesque Irish gentleman registered as "land baron," and Baron O'Keefe he was from that time on.

Othar Wamsley

OTHAR WAMSLEY was working for the Studebaker factory in South Bend, Indiana, when a Chicago realtor selling Montana property found his way there. His descriptions of Montana so impressed Wamsley that he and his wife, Alma, decided to take a gamble. Othar, Alma, and their six-year-old daughter, Geraldine, packed their belongings into a boxcar. They arrived in Hamilton in 1908. Wamsley had done carpentry and studied architecture and trigonometry at night school and by mail. At Studebaker's, he had learned how to finish all kinds of wood. Putting these skills together, Wamsley built an impressive octagonal home advertising his expertise. During the next ten years, Wamsley's career took off. Alma gave piano lessons and took in high school teachers who boarded in three upstairs bedrooms. Then came World War I. The Wamsleys sold all their goods and property, and Othar enlisted. The family was at the depot, Othar bound for boot camp and Geraldine and Alma for California to live with relatives, when Armistice was declared. Although they loved Montana, the Wamsleys had no choice but to move on, but their legacy—the unusual octagonal home*—is a Hamilton landmark.

Bill Fairweather

SOME men just weren't meant for good fortune. Bill Fairweather was a tragic example of luck gone awry. In the company of a party of miners on May 26, 1863, Fairweather panned the first gold at Alder Gulch, setting off the famous stampede. The gulch made him rich, but to Fairweather, the gold meant little. Legend has it that he would ride up and down the streets of Virginia City on his horse, Old Antelope, scattering gold nuggets in the dust. He loved to see the children and the Chinese miners scramble for them. He mixed gold dust in his horse's oats, saying that nothing was too good for Old Antelope, the horse that brought him such good luck. But Fairweather died of hard living at Robber's Roost* in 1875. His pockets were empty, and a bottle of whiskey was his only companion. He was not yet forty years old. A diet of gold dust did Fairweather's horse, Old Antelope, no harm. He long outlived his master, enjoying the Ruby Valley pasture of E. F. Johnson into extreme old age. Fairweather's remains lie in Hillside Cemetery, a windswept burial ground overlooking Alder Gulch, where an iron fence surrounds his grave. A recent marker credits him with the Alder Gulch discovery.

Samuel Lewis

SAMUEL LEWIS settled in Bozeman in 1868, joining a small population of African Americans who came to Montana after the Civil War. Lewis, a native of the West Indies, was a skilled barber, an expert sleight-of-hand performer, and a first-class musician. He established a thriving tonsorial parlor and bathhouse on Main Street. Lewis shared his success with his younger sister, Edmonia, financing her studies abroad. Highly acclaimed as one of the most gifted African American sculptors of the nineteenth century, Edmonia displayed her work at the 1894 Chicago Exposition. In 1889, Lewis transformed his modest home into a fine Queen Anne–style showplace that reveals a high level of architectural sophistication. Its grand and beautifully maintained interior features a frescoed parlor ceiling, a tin ceiling in the kitchen, and ornate woodwork. Completed in 1890, the Lewis residence* was then and is now one of Bozeman's most delightful homes. When Lewis died in 1896, he left an estate valued at twenty-five thousand dollars. It was a well-deserved fortune likely unparalleled by other contemporary African American Montanans.

Tommy Haw

No one knows exactly where Tommy Haw came from, and Tommy himself was too young to remember. Perhaps fate brought him to a restaurant window one morning in 1850. Rancher Tom Orr was in San Francisco on business, and as he sat at a table by the window eating breakfast, he noticed the small Chinese boy, nose to the glass, watching every bite. Orr got up, went outside, and invited the boy to share his meal. The youngster attacked his food, and Orr could tell that he hadn't eaten in a while. Patiently questioning him, Orr discovered that the boy was an orphan, four years old. The boy's manners and politeness impressed him, so Orr took him took his Yreka, California, ranch, where the family welcomed Tommy into the household. Tommy was fifteen in 1864 when Tom Orr and his partner William Poindexter, who had a prosperous business supplying beef to mining camps, decided to trail a herd to Montana. They drove the first cattle and sheep into the Beaverhead Valley, planting the seeds for the famed Poindexter and Orr (P & O) Ranch. Tommy worked on the ranch for many years, saved his wages, and eventually invested in his own cattle and sheep, accumulating quite a fortune. His registered brand was OC, for "Orr's Chinaman." Tommy invested in numerous mining and other enterprises that never quite seemed to pan out, and his fortune dwindled. He died in 1913 and was buried in the Poindexter Cemetery along with his adopted family. Cattle now graze in this historic cemetery.

Wild, Wicked, and
Wonderful Women

Emma Ingalls

THE newspaper Emma Ingalls and her husband founded, the *Kalispell Inter Lake,* allowed her to editorialize for civic reform. A rival editor said she was a "clever and interesting writer who occasionally wielded a caustic pen." Ingalls was also a pioneer homesteader, the first to irrigate in the Flathead Valley, and managed by herself when her husband's health failed. One of the first two women elected to the Montana legislature in 1917, Ingalls introduced the national suffrage amendment when it came before the Montana House for ratification. Returning for a second term, Ingalls sponsored the bill establishing Mountain View Vocational School for Girls. Until that time, courts remanded both boys and girls to the state reform school at Miles City. Separation of boys and girls was an important step in the care of delinquent juveniles. Ingalls was the first woman to work with the Bureau of Child and Animal Protection, chairing the northwest district under Governor Joseph Dixon. Despite her accomplishments, Ingalls believed her life was unremarkable. "God put me on his anvil and hammered me into shape," she once said. "The things that seemed so hard to bear at the time have proven to be the stepping stones to a larger, richer life."

Maggie Hathaway

✳ ACCLAIMED for translating ethics into action, Maggie Hathaway blazed a long and noteworthy trail as one of the first two
women elected to the Montana legislature in 1917. Hathaway cam-
paigned vigorously for women's suffrage before the 1914 election,
traveling just as many thousands of miles as Jeannette Rankin. She
did the same for Prohibition in 1916, speaking in every neighborhood in Ravalli County. During her two legislative terms, Hathaway's
fellow male legislators affectionately called her "Mrs. Has-Her-Way."
Hathaway drafted the Montana's Mother's Pension Bill, allowing
women compensation when their spouses failed to support their
children. She fought to create the Child Welfare Division and
made the impassioned speech that won the eight-hour workday for
women. In 1918, with nearly 10 percent of Montana's men serving
in World War I, Hathaway spoke on behalf of grain farmers, offering women's services to harvest their crops. She employed women
only on her "manless" ranch so more men could join the armed
services. She gathered apples as well as ballots, hitched up her own
plow, and turned furrows as straight as any man. A male legislator said of the diminutive redhead, "She is the biggest man in the
House." Hathaway served three terms in the legislature and, like
her colleague Emma Ingalls, earned the respect of, and courtesy
from, her male colleagues.

Evelyn Cameron

✳ TERRY, Montana, on the state's eastern edge, was home to
Evelyn Cameron, a talented woman who documented the
homesteading era and Montana outdoors with shutter, lens, and
expert eye. Cameron's photographs capture the spirit of the West just
as surely as Charlie Russell's famous paintings define Montana cowboys. Cameron came to Montana from England with her husband to

raise polo ponies to ship back to the British Isles. Although that idea failed, Cameron learned the art of photography and set about capturing life on the eastern plains. She died in 1928, but years later, in the late 1970s, Time-Life books editor Donna Lucey stumbled upon 1,800 photo negatives and 2,700 original prints stored for half a century in the Terry basement of Janet Williams, Cameron's best friend. Lucey studied Cameron's meticulous diaries and photographs to research her book, *Photographing Montana 1894–1928: The Life and Works of Evelyn Cameron*. Published in 2000, it revealed many of Cameron's photos for the first time. If you visit Terry, be sure to stop at the Prairie County Museum and visit the Cameron ranch site.

Julia Tuell

MONTANA'S Northern Cheyennes and the Sioux of South Dakota in the early twentieth century are the subjects of Julia Tuell's little-known photographic legacy. Through her camera lens, Tuell recorded details she must have known would someday be valued. She was sixteen in 1901 when she married forty-three-year-old teacher P. V. Tuell. The couple headed west, where P. V. had a job teaching Indian children. By 1906, on the Northern Cheyenne Reservation at Lame Deer, Tuell had begun collecting images of the Plains Indians at a time of agonizing change when traditional skills were still part of reservation life. With her own small children in tow, Tuell captured intimate details: women scraping hides, dogs hitched to travois, chiefs in full regalia, and children at play. Later, on the Sioux reservations of South Dakota, Tuell continued her photographic journal in a Model T, her camera on the seat. Her photographs parallel those of Evelyn Cameron, who so beautifully documented eastern Montana homesteading. But Tuell's images capture a different perspective of those who saw their lives turned upside down with the tilling of the prairie sod. Her work is a pictorial tribute to the people of the plains. You can find Tuell's poignant photographs in Dan Aadland's book, *Women and Warriors of the Plains.*

Stagecoach Mary

STAGECOACH Mary Fields, a colorful character familiar to early-day residents of Cascade, packed a Smith and Wesson, smoked cigars, weighed two hundred pounds, and stood six feet tall. Cowboy artist Charlie Russell sketched her, and actor Gary Cooper wrote about her fondly for *Ebony* magazine in 1959. Fields, born a slave in Tennessee, made her way to Ohio, where she befriended the Ursuline sisters in Toledo. Mother Superior Amadeus Dunn and Fields became good friends. In 1884, Mother Amadeus came to Montana to work among the Blackfeet. When Mother Amadeus fell victim to pneumonia, Fields came west to nurse her friend back to health. Fields became a fixture at St. Peter's Mission,* where she did all the heavy freighting, bringing supplies through blizzards and dangerous situations. Fields was fearless and had quite a temper. After an altercation, Bishop John Brondel of Helena ordered the Ursulines to banish her. But Mother Amadeus appealed to federal authorities, securing her as the driver of the mail route between Cascade and the mission. Fields became the second woman stage driver in the United States. For eight years she drove the stage. When the horses couldn't get through, she carried the mail on her back. Fields died in 1914, a pioneer who helped tame the West, beloved by all, except perhaps the Catholic bishop.

Fannie Sperry Steele

FAMED bronc buster Fannie Sperry Steele competed in rodeos until 1925. Then she and her husband bought a dude ranch near Lincoln. After her husband died in 1940, Steele ran the ranch by herself for another twenty-five years. She was one of the first women to receive a packer's license and well into her sixties spent long days in the saddle guiding hunters into rough country. She stocked Meadow Creek before environmental concerns were fashionable, packing six horses with cans of fish over treacherous terrain, stopping at every stream to keep the water cool. She broke her own horses and at the end of the season trailed her twenty-five pintos seventy miles across the Continental Divide to winter pasture. In 1974, at age eighty-seven, Steele could no longer live alone and had to move from the ranch. The worst part for her was leaving her beloved string of pintos behind. In 1975, Steele was honored as was one of the first of three women inducted into the Rodeo Hall of Fame. A few years later, at ninety, Steele summed up her life: "To the yesterdays that are gone, to the cowboys I used to know, to the bronc busters that rode beside me, to the horses beneath me (sometimes), I take off my hat. I wouldn't have missed one minute of it." Steele died in 1983. She was the quintessential Montana woman: determined, gritty, and independent of spirit.

Bridget Sullivan

BRIDGET SULLIVAN was seventeen when she came to New York from Ireland aboard the *S.S. Republic*. In 1889, she took employment as a live-in maid for a prominent family in Fall River, Massachusetts. It was a difficult family to work for because the wealthy head of the household was something of a miser and the wife was very demanding. The morning of August 4, 1892, changed the course of Sullivan's life when her employers, Andrew and Abby Borden, were viciously hacked to death with an ax. Their daughter Lizzie, charged with the murders, stood trial in one of the most famous courtroom dramas of all time. Sullivan, who was in the home at the time of the murders, was a key witness and took the stand at every phase of the trial. Some speculate that Sullivan's testimony was odd, and that perhaps she did not tell all she knew.

Lizzie was acquitted. Sullivan eventually settled in Anaconda, where she was the longtime maid of the Judge George Winston family. In 1905, Sullivan married a man with the same last name, and the couple lived quietly. She never spoke of the crime but reportedly confessed on her deathbed in 1948 that Lizzie paid her for her evasive testimony.

Ella Knowles Haskell

ELLA KNOWLES faced formidable obstacles in pursuing a career in law. Upon statehood in 1889, a statute prohibited women from passing the bar. After much debate, Montana lawmakers amended the statute, thinking a woman could never pass anyhow. Knowles astounded them and passed with flying colors. She became the first woman licensed to practice law in Montana. But acquiring clients was another matter. She tried in vain to convince Helena merchants to hire her as their bill collector. Finally, one merchant challenged her to retrieve all the umbrellas his rich customers had borrowed on rainy days. She returned every one. The merchant paid her two quarters, her first fee; she kept them for the rest of her life. Knowles practiced law until 1892, and then she ran on the Populist ticket for attorney general, the second woman in the nation to run for that office. She didn't win—likely because women couldn't vote. But her opponent, Henri Haskell, appointed her assistant attorney general after he won the election. Later, they married and then divorced. Knowles practiced law in Butte until she died in 1911. In 1997, Ella Knowles Haskell was inducted into the Capitol's Gallery of Outstanding Montanans.

Chicago Joe

JOSEPHINE "CHICAGO JOE" HENSLEY was one of Helena's several well-known madams. Her infamous Coliseum Theatre in the 1880s and early 1890s carried a payroll of one thousand dollars a week. Hensley earned her nickname because of the attractive girls she imported from Chicago to work for her. At the height of her success, Hensley owned more than two hundred thousand dollars worth of real estate, helped many financially, contributed to local causes, and anonymously educated two younger sisters, two nieces, a nephew, and a half brother. In later years, she cut quite a figure presiding over her cash register wearing an enormous Elizabethan collar and a dark, flowing velvet robe of purple or green, her ample waist encircled by a jewel-studded golden sash. Jewels sparkled everywhere on her person that they could be pinned. Hensley died of cirrhosis of the liver following surgery in 1899. E. W. Toole, brother of the governor, rode behind her coffin in an open carriage, an unheard-of gesture. Hensley's generosity was admirable, and so was her intelligence. She accomplished what few others could, especially when you consider her handicap: she could neither read nor write. Hensley's remains lie in an unmarked grave beneath modern-day Robinson Park, where the Catholic cemetery used to be.

Carrie Nation 1

In 1910, the hatchet-wielding, bar-smashing temperance crusader Carrie Nation came to Butte. At that time, Butte had 275 saloons; even Mayor Charles Nevin owned a bar. Booze joints in nearby Anaconda sported signs that read, "All Nations welcome except Carrie," while reformers welcomed her with open arms. Onlookers cheered as the stout sixty-three-year-old Mrs. Nation, with a flourish and a crowd in tow, charged down the length of Butte's notorious Pleasant Alley.* She had some difficulty communicating with the resident prostitutes because few of them spoke English. At the end of the alley back on Mercury Street, she burst into the Irish World, a well-known parlor house, and met her match in madam May Maloy. The two got into a scuffle, and Maloy booted Mrs. Nation out the door with a well-placed kick. She emerged with her bonnet askew, suffering from a wrenched elbow. It was a moment Maloy's patrons savored, and they celebrated with drinks all around. Thus Carrie Nation made not so much as a single convert in Butte. In fact, Butte likes to claim that Maloy's was the last saloon Carrie Nation ever set foot in. While that's not exactly true, it may have marked a turning point in her career.

Carrie Nation 2

AFTER Carrie Nation, the famous hatchet-toting, bar-smashing temperance leader, visited Butte in 1910, she made a swing deeper into Montana. Nation stood nearly six feet tall, weighed in at 175 pounds, and was an altogether formidable-looking woman. She claimed that her calling to promote temperance came from divine ordination and described herself as "a bulldog running along at the feet of Jesus, barking at what He doesn't like." She came to Helena to speak at the invitation of the local Women's Christian Temperance Union. The women expressed some concern that Nation might say or do something shocking as she often did. The crowd, however, was small, and Nation made no converts in the Capital City. And in Kalispell, when she delivered her gospel message in front of the infamous Heller Saloon,* she and owner August Heller exchanged heated words. Heller declared that he might own a saloon, but at least it was honest work and he was not a "grafter" like Carrie Nation. Nation took her Bible and her hatchet souvenirs and left Montana for places where converts were easier to come by. She had little time left for converts, though. She died in 1911.

Marie Gibson

SIXTEEN-YEAR-OLD Marie Gibson's marriage was on the rocks, so she joined her parents on their homestead near Havre in

1914. With the encouragement of neighbors, including legendary cowboy Long George Francis, Gibson began trick riding in local fairs and rodeos for prize money to help support her children. Her professional debut came in 1917 at Havre's Great Stampede. She married for a second time in 1919. Her husband, rodeo veteran Tom Gibson, retired to the family homestead and Marie went on to travel widely, busting broncs overseas and back East. During a performance in England, she so charmed the Prince of Wales that he presented her with a prize horse. Gibson earned many titles, including World Champion Cowgirl Bronc Rider in 1924 and 1927. In 1933, Gibson made a successful ride on a wild bronc in Idaho. The horse was still bucking as the pickup man approached to take her off. The two horses collided, and Gibson's horse lost his balance and fell on her, fatally fracturing her skull. Her hobbled stirrups prevented her from kicking free. Her son Lucien, then twenty-three, rushed to her aid, but it was too late. Gibson is buried in Havre, where locals rightfully claim her as one of their own.

May Butler

LONGTIME teacher May Butler lived her entire life in the quaint carpenter gothic home* her father built in 1879, high upon the hillside at the south end of Helena's Benton Avenue. You can see its peaked roof with the gingerbread trim from several vantage points around town. It was (and still is) accessible only by a series of steep stairs from the street. Fortunately, Butler never had to carry groceries or packages up the stairs. Her father ingeniously constructed a slide leading from the rear alley above the house to the back door. The delivery wagons pulled up to the slide, placed the items on it, and with a gentle push they ended up at the kitchen door. Miss Butler taught in many one-room rural schoolhouses in Montana and at several different public schools in Helena. She had tiny hands and feet that somehow didn't match her three-hundred-pound frame. "But when you were little," a former student declared, "and saw that hand coming at you, it looked huge!" Miss Butler was strict, but she was very caring and a lot of fun. She was ambidextrous and amazed her students by writing on the blackboard simultaneously with both hands. Children often brought her homemade breads and jellies. She would cut the bread, open the jelly, lay it out on her desk, and invite everyone to have some. But she always added one condition, "Save the biggest piece for me!"

Greenough Sisters

As the first national professional rodeo organization formed in 1929 with men and women as members, Marge and Alice Greenough of Red Lodge bridged the final transition between the old West and the modern era. Their father, "Packsaddle Ben" Greenough, was a local character who guided seasonal packtrips into the local wilderness. The Greenoughs kept horses by the hundreds. Ben expected his children to gentle the wildest horses in a rock-littered corral. "Nobody," Marge reflected, "could get bucked off in those rocks and live." His method was effective. Alice rode her first bronco in public at Forsyth in 1919 when she was just seventeen. Marge, five years younger, won the half-mile cowgirl race at the Red Lodge rodeo in 1924. Marge later rode bareback broncos and steers while Alice did exceptional trick riding. Both sisters eventually rode bucking broncos and bulls and won many championships. The Greenough sisters were refined, well-spoken, and dressed like ladies when they were not riding. They carried their sewing machine on the road and made their own clothes. They endured the same struggles as their male counterparts, suffered the same injuries, and rode the same horses. The Greenough sisters, their saddle-bronc-champion brother Turk, and other family members helped bring the professional Home of Champions Rodeo to Red Lodge. After Alice and Marge retired, they moved to Arizona, where they were involved in the film industry, but Montanans know they hailed from Red Lodge.

Sarah Bickford

VIRGINIA CITY businesswoman Sarah Bickford was born into slavery. Her parents were sold when she was very young, and she never saw them again. After the Civil War, Sarah went to live with an aunt in Tennessee. She came west at age fifteen in the employ of the John L. Murphy family. Judge Murphy served briefly as associate justice in the territorial Supreme Court at Virginia City. Sarah took take care of the Murphys' children on the journey west. The Murphys soon returned to the states, but Sarah stayed, working as a chambermaid in a Virginia City hotel. She often told how a co-worker found a poke of gold dust worth fifteen hundred dollars left by a hotel guest. She tracked him down and returned it, and the miserly miner gave her a reward of twenty-five cents. Sarah married a miner and had three children, but by the 1880s, her entire family had died. In 1881, Sarah married Stephen Bickford, a miner and owner of the Virginia City Water Company. With Stephen, she had two girls and a boy who grew up listening to poignant stories about their mother's first set of children. When Stephen died in 1900, Sarah took over the water company. She kept her office in Virginia City's famous Hangman's Building until her death in 1931. Sarah Bickford was one of the first women, and perhaps the only black woman in the nation, to own a utility.

Mary Gleim

EVERY western town had its houses of ill repute. In Montana, a few significant remnants of these colorful businesses survive, including the Dumas* in Butte, Big Dorothy's* in Helena, and two of Mary Gleim's West Front Street brothels* in Missoula. Gleim was a flamboyant character who operated eight "female boarding houses" in Missoula's red light district, where railroad men patronized its honky tonks and saloons. Gleim's splashy career included conviction in 1894 for the attempted murder of a rival. Her prison record notes that she arrived at the prison in Deer Lodge* to serve her sentence dressed to the nines in a "complete outfit." During her prison term, another female prisoner viciously stabbed her, and Gleim never quite recovered from the attack. Reputedly a smuggler of laces, diamonds, opium, and Chinese railroad workers, the mountainous madam weighed three hundred pounds. She was a formidable opponent and a match for any man. "Mother Gleim," as she was also known, operated brothels until her death in 1914. She left an estate of one hundred thousand dollars. Her former brothels, both nicely renovated and adaptively reused as businesses, add to the interesting history of the 200 block of West Front Street. According to her wishes, Gleim's tombstone—unlike all the others in the Missoula city cemetery—faces the railroad tracks. This way, Gleim could bid farewell to the many railroad men who were her customers.

Epitaphs

Virginia City's Boot Hill

✦ OVERLOOKING Virginia City are five stark tombstones mark-ing the graves of five accused road agents, hanged by the vigilantes in 1864. The cemetery, known as Boot Hill, was the town's first burial ground. But the stigma attached to the five outlaws buried there was so great that, within a few years, Hillside Cemetery was established nearby where most families moved the graves of their law-abiding loved ones. The five outlaws' graves lay unidenti-fied on Boot Hill until 1907 when Mayor James Walker decided to mark them. Legend has it that he took a few men and some whiskey up the hill in the dark of night. Following eyewitness A. B. Davis's description of the order of the five burials, the men began to dig where they thought Clubfoot George Lane was buried. Sure enough, between swigs and before long they unearthed some remains. By lantern light, they readily identified Lane's misshapen foot bone. Thus Davis's recollection had been correct, and Walker marked the graves accordingly. The mayor kept the foot as a souvenir. After his death, the family donated the grisly object, with a piece of sock still attached, to Virginia City's Thompson-Hickman Museum. You can view it there today.

Dalton Memorial

✴ BESIDES the five road agents' graves atop Virginia City's Boot Hill, there is a poignant memorial to Clara and William Dalton, who came to Bannack with the first Fisk train in 1862. The Daltons (unrelated to the infamous Dalton gang) and their four children soon moved to Virginia City, where nineteen-year-old Mathilda became very ill with typhoid. She recovered, but her mother and father also became ill, and both died within two weeks of each other. Mathilda married and left Montana. Late in her life, Mathilda provided information about Bannack's infamous Sheriff Henry Plummer. In 1918, Mathilda wrote that the Plummer family had been the Daltons' neighbors back in Maine in the 1840s. When her father followed the rush to California in the 1850s, he came across Henry Plummer and knew him well. When the Dalton family came to Bannack, Mathilda's father was astonished to again meet Plummer on the street. But the sheriff refused to acknowledge him. Dalton felt this behavior confirmed Plummer's dishonesty. He told Mathilda that Plummer, once an honest man, became a terrible discredit to his family back East. The Daltons' graves were unmarked until the twentieth century when Mathilda's children visited Virginia City and placed the current monument on Boot Hill.

Charley's Boot

✴ AMONG the many diaries kept by emigrants along the Bozeman Trail, one stands out as the most poignant, a tragic reminder of the real risks early travelers faced. William Thomas left his Illinois farm in 1866 after his wife and twin daughters died of pneumonia. William took his seven-year-old son, Charley, and a driver, Joseph Schultz, to join William's brother George in Montana Territory. They traveled in a prairie schooner, drawn by a pair of five-hundred-dollar mules. William's diary is strangely full of forebodings and once, remarking on his emotions gazing at distant mountains, wrote, "cold chills run through my blood." He was right to feel apprehensive. William's party broke off from the main group to travel Sawyer's Cutoff, and on August 23, 1866, they camped near the Yellowstone at present-day Greycliff. The next day, other travelers came upon their campsite, the fire still warm. William had thirteen arrows in his body; Charley had three. Both had been scalped. Schultz, whose body was found in the river, had apparently been fishing when the attack occurred. William's diary was found in his pocket. Indians took or destroyed nearly everything except a few books, a family Bible, Charley's hunting knife, and only one of his small worn boots, now part of the museum collections of the Montana Historical Society. The other boot was never found.

Gebo Cemetery*

LOCATED next to the abandoned townsite of Gebo, the cemetery overlooks the Gebo mines and marks the passing of birth and life in one of many of Montana's boom-and-bust communities. Named after an early miner who opened the first mines there, Gebo enjoyed some prosperity with a population fluctuating from five hundred to one thousand while the coal mines operated from 1899 to 1912. The town in its heyday included a drugstore, café, rooming house, confectionery, laundry, barbershop, post office, newspaper, and five bars. The mine closed in 1912, and Gebo was then nearly abandoned, many of its residents removing to nearby Fromberg. Many of Gebo's buildings were also moved there. Only a few residents remained in Gebo into the Great Depression. In 1987, the remaining buildings, foundations, mine adits, and cisterns were razed for public safety. The Montana Department of State Lands backfilled, graded, and replanted the area. Some two hundred graves dot the cemetery, many marked with wooden crosses and pink or gray granite tombstones. Some have iron crosses. Several graves date to the period 1901–1918; many date to the 1930s. Today, residents of Fromberg and descendants of Gebo's citizens occasionally still visit the cemetery, the only reminder of a once-vibrant community.

Peel's Tombstone

LANGFORD PEEL was a desperado. Armed with a brace of guns and a hefty reputation as a gunslinger and a card shark, he came to Last Chance with his sometime business partner John Bull in the summer of 1867. The two got into an argument, and Peel drew his gun. Bull had no weapon on him, so he asked Peel if he could get his gun. Peel let him go. When Bull came back into the bar, he didn't wait for Peel to draw his weapon, but killed him outright. Peel was buried in Helena's City Cemetery, where Central School* is today. A tombstone, five feet tall and expertly carved, marked his grave. The curious inscription read in part, "Vengeance is mine, sayeth the lord. I know that my redeemer liveth." Peel's contemporaries viewed this inscription not as religious but rather as a curse against Peel's murderer. It worked. About ten years later, Peel was avenged when John Bull was killed in a saloon fight. Peel's grave was among the many moved to Benton Avenue Cemetery* during the construction of Central School in 1875. Wilbur Fisk Sanders took Peel's tombstone to save it from vandalism and stashed it in his attic. There it lay until its rediscovery in 1927 by new owners of the Sanders' old home. They gave the mining-camp relic to the Montana Historical Society. It remains in the collection today.

Forgotten Pioneers

CHINESE immigrants came to America with the first California gold rushes in the 1840s. They were among the first waves of frontier adventurers who came to Montana in the 1860s seeking pay dirt in the rocky gulches at Bannack, Virginia City, and

Last Chance. Despite anti-Chinese legislation and racial discrimination, they settled in towns across Montana and contributed to the settlement of the American West. Chinese workers laid the tracks of the Northern Pacific in the 1880s, and they blasted the rock to build the Mullan Tunnel, making rail travel possible across the Great Divide. Chinese pioneers operated businesses, provided services, and paid local taxes. The Chinese population dwindled into the twentieth century as the predominantly male residents returned home to China or died leaving no family. Many Chinese neighborhoods fell victim to urban renewal in the 1970s, erasing all evidence of their presence. The Wah Chong Tai* and Mai Wah Noodle Parlor* buildings in Butte are among the few surviving landmarks. One of the nation's largest industrial urban centers, Butte supported Montana's largest Chinese population, which stood at 2,532 in 1910. The Mah Wah Society maintains the two landmarks and serves as caretaker of Butte's rich Asian heritage. The remains of scores of Chinese lie among prairie grass and prickly pear in a wind-swept field outside the tended grounds of Forestvale Cemetery* in Helena. These few remnants are the only physical reminders of a forgotten people who once comprised nearly 10 percent of Montana's territorial population.

A. K. Prescott

ALTHOUGH Montana's first communities had skilled stonemasons, there were no craftsmen who made tombstones. In the early cemeteries, white marble slabs are usually the oldest kinds of grave markers, and these were often custom made, but they were imported from elsewhere. A. K. Prescott came to Butte by stagecoach from the mining camp of Rico, Colorado, where he had established the town's first store. Once at Butte, Prescott heard from a bereaved husband that in all of Montana Territory, he could not buy a finished headstone for his wife's grave. Prescott took this information to heart, returned east, hired two stonecutters, and returned to Butte, where he established Montana's first local tombstone business. Soon he opened a branch in Helena. Prescott built up a huge business, traveling all over the territory to communities with graveyards filled with wooden markers. He would set up temporary shop, take orders, cut the tombstones, and then move on to the next place. Many of Prescott's markers are still upright and readable in Montana's oldest cemeteries. When competitors opened businesses in the later 1880s, Prescott invested in sheep ranching, made a fortune, and generously helped others, with his financial backing, to do the same.

Home of Peace*

AMONG the ethnic groups that came in significant numbers to Montana with the 1860s gold rush were Jewish merchants and service providers. Montana's first Hebrew Benevolent Society organized at Virginia City around 1865. The only cultural remnant this vibrant population left there is a Hebrew Cemetery, now obliterated, but noted on Virginia City's first plat map. Most of the Jewish population moved on to Helena around 1866 and played a significant role in Helena's early economy. Jews were bankers, lawyers, business owners, and cattlemen. The Home of Peace, the small cemetery adjacent to Capital High School, is the resting place of more than 250 of our early settlers. It is Montana's oldest active Jewish Cemetery, founded in 1867, and it is the oldest cemetery in Helena still in use. The first person buried there was Emanuel Blum, who died in 1865. At the time of his death, there was no Jewish burial ground, so he was first buried in the city cemetery where Central School* is today. When Helena's Hebrew Benevolent Society established the Home of Peace two years later, Blum was reinterred. His final resting place is today unmarked. Also buried at the Home of Peace are Ben Ezekiel and Solomon Content. Ezekiel was one of the original members of the Virginia City vigilantes. Content was the owner of Content's Corner, one of the 1860s architectural anchors along Wallace Street in Virginia City.

Pete Zortman Comes Home

OLIVER PETER ZORTMAN came west in 1888, lured by gold discovered in central Montana's Little Rocky Mountains. He struck it rich several times, ran a cyanide mill, and left his name on the town of Zortman. He was part of an elite group—one of very few to leave the Little Rockies with a small fortune in gold. He joined the Masons in Chinook and eventually ended up in Big Timber, where he died of cancer in 1933, penniless. No stone marked his final resting place, but the local newspaper that documented his passing mentioned that he was buried in a hand-dug pauper's grave. A few years ago, Zortman residents decided to honor their namesake. It was no small task to discover Zortman's unmarked resting place. A long search led to Zortman's membership in the Masons. The leather-bound records of the Big Timber Masonic Lodge offered details of Zortman's funeral. With permission from Zortman's relatives, several veterinarians, a Chinook undertaker, cemetery workers, and assorted Zortman residents oversaw the exhumation. The remains of Pete Zortman surfaced from the chocolate soil in Big Timber's Mountain View Cemetery with some difficulty. Water from an irrigation ditch immediately flooded the hole as the backhoe dug. Three feet of muck was removed, and pieces of the coffin and Zortman began to surface. The yellowed bones were placed in a newly made pine coffin and loaded onto a truck. On August 27, 2005, a vintage hearse carried the pine box to the Zortman Cemetery. A smattering of relatives and most of the town of Zortman attended the graveside services. Pete Zortman was home.

Episodes

A Persistent Myth

STORIES abound across the West about "Chinese tunnels" beneath the buildings and streets of cities and towns. According to Priscilla Wegars of the University of Idaho, a foremost authority on Asian culture in the West, there is overwhelming evidence that "Chinese tunnels" are nothing more than myths. Not a single "Chinese tunnel" has ever been identified. While it is true that Chinese businesses, opium dens, and even living quarters are sometimes found in basement spaces, these in no way can be called "tunnels." The Chinese were often targets of discrimination, but they did not live underground because of persecution as many believe. Basements were simply cheaper to rent than rooms above ground. Further, the basements of nineteenth- and early-twentieth-century business blocks frequently had arched doorways leading to sidewalk vaults. These were storage or delivery areas. Lit by glass blocks turned purple with age, these mysterious vaults had nothing to do with the Chinese. Tunnel systems beneath downtown areas in Helena, Butte, Missoula, Bozeman, and elsewhere do exist; they served as steam-heat delivery systems. While sometimes steam tunnels served clandestine purposes, particularly for alcohol delivery during Prohibition, these passageways cannot be termed "Chinese tunnels." Finally, in all settlements where mining was extensive, hand-dug tunnels often remain beneath residential neighborhoods and downtown business areas. Miners of all ethnic groups dug tunnels, and there is nothing that makes a tunnel exclusively Chinese.

Cinnabar

✳ A FEW buried foundation walls are all that mark the place where the town of Cinnabar once hosted a presidential entourage. Situated on the flats between the Yellowstone River and the Gallatin Mountains in the shadows of the famous Electric Peak and Devil's Slide, Cinnabar took root in 1883. As the Northern Pacific Railroad's terminus of its Yellowstone Park branch, the town, four miles north of the park's entrance, was a lonely stopping place for some twenty years. In 1902, the Northern Pacific extended its line to the new town of Gardiner, where the monumental entrance arch* to Yellowstone Park was under construction. But the depot and visitor services were as yet nonexistent when, in May 1903, President Theodore Roosevelt planned a preseason tour and dedication of the entrance arch. Cinnabar was the only place to locate the nation's portable capital. For sixteen days, Pullman, parlor, and dining cars serving President Roosevelt and White House staff parked along the tracks at Cinnabar. A contingent of secret service men and newspaper writers added to the throng of visitors. The cavalry stationed in the area made their horses available for fishing trips and sightseeing, and stagecoaches offered excursions into the park. Cinnabar's shabby buildings and antiquated services were a far cry from the nation's sophisticated capital. Associated Press official Harry Colman remarked, "Well, thank goodness, this blooming town will be wiped off the map when we leave. It's a mystery to me how it ever got on in the first place." Once the presidential cars sped down the tracks, Cinnabar's businesses moved to Gardiner, and that brief moment in time was Cinnabar's last hurrah.

Prairie Figs

✳ JOHNNY GRANT, founder of the Grant-Kohrs Ranch,* was
the son of the factor at the Hudson's Bay Company fort near
Pocatello, Idaho. Johnny's memoirs, wonderfully edited by Lyndel
Meikle under the title *Very Close to Trouble,* are full of interesting
historical anecdotes. One memorable footnote recounts the story
of a green Missourian who came into the fort store. Johnny's father
decided to have some sport with the unsuspecting traveler. Casto-
rums are beaver glands that trappers used as bait. There were a
number of these foul objects hanging in the store. The Missourian
asked what they were. "Prairie figs," replied the elder Grant. "Are
they good to eat?" asked the Missourian. "For those who like them,"
answered Grant. "Can I taste one?" Grant answered, "Certainly."
The traveler picked a good full one and bit into it. The putrid gum
and oil ran down the sides of his mouth, and Johnny recalled how
comical it was to see the man making faces trying to spit it out.
For some time he couldn't speak. Finally he said, "They might be
good for those who like them, but I declare I do not." This comical
story and the singular name suggests that Prairie Figs would make
a terrific name for a modern-day band!

Sleeping Giant

✳ THE Beartooth Mountains in Yellowstone County were at
one time not the only mountains in Montana so named. A
range in Lewis and Clark County was also known as the Beartooth
Mountains for a famous jagged peak that resembled the twin tusks
in the open jaw of a giant bear. Lewis and Clark described the spectacular formation in mid-July 1805, and the Bear Tooth became
a well-known landmark. But in February 1878, a hunting party
noticed a rumbling of the earth. The shaking was quickly over, and
supposing it to be a mild earthquake, they forgot about it and went

on their way. But when they reached the Bear Tooth, they discovered one of its tusks—a perpendicular mass of rock three hundred feet in circumference and five hundred feet high—had dislodged and tumbled down the mountainside, leveling an entire forest. The loss of the tooth left only one grim peak, and the landmark Bear Tooth was forgotten. The mountain peak's resemblance to a stout sleeping figure so familiar today was not actually noted until 1893. The *Helena Daily Herald* reported that a visitor unfamiliar with the local landscape observed that the mountain formation looked like a sleeping burgomaster. It soon became known as the Sleeping Giant. The giant's nose is the remaining tusk of the Bear Tooth.

Butte Explosion

BUTTE has had its share of mining disasters and has mourned its share of fallen heroes. But no disaster precipitated more fire protection improvements than an explosion that occurred on January 15, 1895. Butte firemen answered a fire call in the South Butte warehouse of the Royal Milling Company. The firemen did not know that tons of blasting powder had been illegally stored in the nearby Kenyon-Connell Commercial Company and Butte Hardware Company warehouses. Flames reached the powder, and the first terrific explosion blew the metal roof of the Kenyon-Connell building one hundred feet in the air, hurling bystanders and the entire Butte fire department to their deaths. As passersby rushed to aid victims, two more blasts turned iron bars and metal pipes stored in the warehouse into deadly missiles that found targets as distant as a mile from the explosions. Searing oil rained down on the crowd. Sidewalks throughout Butte all the way to Walkerville glistened with broken glass from shattered windows. Authorities counted at least fifty-nine dead and more than one hundred injured, but Butte's transient population and the complete annihilation of some victims suggested the toll was much higher. Only the Speculator Mine disaster in 1917 eclipsed this horrendous calamity.

Fire!

✴ IN 1910, a terrible fire at Marysville precipitated a heated exchange in the Helena newspaper. Helena firemen rode a special train to Marysville to help fight the fire. Helenans who rode the train reported that the citizens of Marysville stood and watched their commercial district burn. While merchants carried goods out of threatened buildings, looters helped themselves. The crowd broke down the doors of the saloons and passed the whiskey around. Helenans claimed there were wild scenes of hilarious intoxication. Maryville citizens, however, told a different tale. While they thanked the Helena fire department for its help, they claimed the fire was already under control when the train arrived and that the firemen knew there was a water shortage, yet they brought only a hose to fight the fire. Had they brought some apparatus to throw water or chemicals on the fire, the entire west side could have been saved. The only intoxicated persons were a couple of hoboes and a few Helenans, and any looters were promptly arrested. The damage to Marysville's reputation, charged its citizens, was worse than that caused by the fire. There was probably some truth to both sides.

Women Win the Right to Vote

✴ WHEN miners discovered gold at Grasshopper Creek in 1862, women in the United States could not vote, could not work in most professions, and could not attend most colleges. The road to women's suffrage was long and full of bumps. Sometimes it seemed that the obstacles were insurmountable. Between 1869 and 1871, seven western legislatures considered giving women the vote.

Montana's was not one of them. Men dominated Montana Territory seven to one, and they long resisted the idea. Victories for Montana women were slow in coming. There were but a few small steps along the way. In 1887, a constitutional amendment to Montana's territorial constitution gave tax-paying women the right to vote in school elections and hold elected positions as school trustees and county superintendants. But equality stopped there. After statehood, women's suffrage bills repeatedly came before the Montana legislature and failed. In 1911, Missoula social worker Jeannette Rankin addressed the legislature. "Men and women," she said, "are like right and left hands; it doesn't make sense not to use both." The bill again failed, but this time Montana suffragists did not give up so easily. They began to organize with Rankin as their leader. In 1913, Governor Samuel Stewart took up the cause of suffrage, and the amendment finally passed with only two dissenting votes in each house of the legislature. Suffragists—never "suffragette," which women considered a demeaning term—traveled thousands of miles across Montana, distributing leaflets and making speeches on every street corner. On November 3, 1914, Montana men went to the polls and granted women the right to cast their ballots. Montana became the sixth state to empower women with the right to vote.

First Elected Women

NOT all women favored suffrage. Those against it, called "Antis," argued that no woman could possibly find time for politics without neglecting her family. Harriet Sanders, wife of pioneer attorney and politician Wilbur Fisk Sanders, countered the opposition, saying that suffrage made women better mothers. Better mothers kept better homes, and their children were better educated. Better homes and educated children in turn improved the nation. Women had much work to do. Montana women helped elect Jeannette Rankin to Congress in 1916, four years before women achieved national suffrage. But other equally significant victories overshadowed Rankin's election. Not only did Montanans send the first woman to Congress in that historic election, they also elected the first two women to the Montana House of Representatives and the first woman superintendent of public instruction. The first women legislators, Emma Ingalls of Flathead County and Maggie Smith Hathaway of Ravalli County, both championed the cause of women's suffrage and spoke out for the disenfranchised. As Ingalls and Hathaway took the seats they earned in the Montana House in 1917, they became the voices of many more than the voters who elected them, especially children and their welfare. And Flathead County's May Trumper defeated three men in the race for school superintendent. Together these women represented the ribbon at the end of the finish line in a long and hard-won race.

Eloped!

HERE'S an interesting story about a Helena bride who was married twice within a couple of months. Her father was Nicholas Kessler, Helena brewer and brickmaker. Kessler met Captain George Cochran, who served under Kessler's command in the First Regiment of Montana volunteers in the Philippines during the 1899 Insurrection. After the war, Cochran was stationed at Fort Harrison. Kessler thought that Cochran would be the perfect son-in-law. So on his deathbed in 1901, Kessler stipulated in his will that his daughter Tillie would inherit her share of the family fortune only if she married Cochran. But Captain Cochran was not Tillie's choice, and in 1903 she eloped with Albert Raleigh, the son of an impoverished Helena merchant. Well, the Kessler brothers got wind of the coming marriage, lay in wait for the newlyweds, and following the ceremony kidnapped Tillie. They took her home to the Kessler residence near the brewery and locked her in her room. The marriage was annulled. Three months later, Tillie married George Cochran, inherited her portion of the Kessler fortune, and the couple had a long life together.

Columbian Exposition

THE 1893 World's Fair, or Columbian Exposition, held in Chicago, commemorated the four-hundredth anniversary of Columbus's discovery of the New World and established Columbus Day as a national holiday. In six months, it attracted 27,539,000 visitors—almost half the total population of the United States at that time. The engineering highlight of the exposition was the first Ferris wheel. It was Chicago's answer to the Eiffel Tower, the landmark of the 1889 Paris Exhibition. Pennsylvania bridge builder George W. Ferris created the wheel to hold thirty-six wooden cars that could hold sixty people each. The original Ferris wheel was scrapped in 1906, but it influenced engineering and entertainment around the world. In Montana, children enjoyed one of the early, smaller-scale Ferris wheels at Columbia Gardens in Butte. The Columbian Exposition introduced many new products still familiar today, such as Aunt Jemima syrup, Cream of Wheat, and Juicy Fruit gum. The fair popularized hamburgers and carbonated soda; it introduced ragtime; and its art and architecture influenced the nation for the next twenty years. That influence is particularly evident in the art and architecture of Montana's State Capitol.*

A Travel Advisory

As gold strikes drew the first miners to southwestern Montana, J. L. Campbell published an emigrant's guide for those contemplating the trip west. The small guide underscores how rapid were the changes at this heady time. By the time it appeared in 1864 under the title *Idaho, Six Months in the New Gold Diggings*, it was already outdated. The area it covered, formerly the Territory of Idaho, had now become the Territory of Montana. Campbell's guide includes firsthand information that is a fascinating testament to the grit necessary for western sojourners. Starting his travels in Nebraska, Campbell discusses the routes to follow, lists the camping places, and notes the supplies an outfit of four will need for nine months. He tells the reader to take canned or dried fruit to prevent scurvy. "Safely carry butter in tins and it will be highly prized," he advised, "and eggs packed in bran or oats will greatly add to the luxuriousness of one's table, making camp life more like home." Campbell admonishes those foolhardy enough to believe that placer mining for gold is easy. It involves hard work. "Simply digging for gold is a lottery," he wrote, "in which there are many prizes but very many blanks. Have a good reason for breaking the old moorings before looking for better ones." There is a copy of Campbell's little booklet at the Montana Historical Society's Research Center. It is highly recommended reading for anyone interested in nineteenth-century western adventure.

Silver Lady

MONTANA sent numerous exhibits to the 1893 World's Columbian Exposition in Chicago. But the state's most costly exhibit was a stroke of genius that millions of fair-goers viewed in the Hall of Mines and Mining. A nine-foot statue cast of pure Montana silver symbolized the nation's second-largest silver supplier. Samuel Hauser loaned twelve thousand ounces of Montana silver, and William A. Clark pledged the same. Montana selected justice as its theme but daringly depicted its statue without the customary blindfold. Montana's justice posed with her eyes wide open. It was a clever advertisement for the federal government's recent adoption of both silver and gold bullion in the coinage of its currency. Internationally renowned actress Ada Rehan served as the model, but many were incensed that the model was not from Montana.

The Silver Lady, resting on a base of solid gold, later became the focus of a mystery. Rumor had it that after the fair, someone substituted a silver-painted wooden statue for the real one and returned it to Montana. The wooden replacement lay in the Lewis and Clark County Courthouse* for many years until someone finally cut it up for kindling. The real statue, however, somehow ended up in litigation in Topeka, Kansas. The court ordered it melted down in 1903, and comparable values were returned in cash to interested parties.

Montana

★ FOR more than a century, the true identity of *Lady Liberty*, perched atop the grand dome of the Montana State Capitol,* was a mystery. The seventeen-foot statue showed up at the Helena depot one day in the late 1890s. No one knew who commissioned her, who made her, or where she came from. She arrived on the heels of the disbanding of the scandalous first capitol commission in 1897. The group, charged with contracting for the construction of the state capitol building, planned to inflate prices and divert funds into their own pockets. Summoned to appear before a grand jury, one commission member committed suicide and others burned records, leaving no proof behind. The statue, however, served the next commission well and took her place on the dome. She was always known as *Lady Liberty*. In 2006, Alice Nagle of Hatfield, Pennsylvania, contacted the Montana Historical Society inquiring if her grandfather's copper-clad statue still graced the capitol's dome. It turned out that Alice had a photograph of the work in progress, solving the mystery of *Lady Liberty*. Her grandfather, Edward J. Van Landeghem, was a Belgian artist who trained at the Academy of Fine Arts School in Brussels. He created the statue in his Philadelphia studio. He named her, however, not *Lady Liberty* but *Montana*, and so after more than a century of relative anonymity, her origins are known and we can call her by her rightful name.

Capitol Hill

AFTER Helena defeated Anaconda in the vitriolic capital election of 1894, the permanent title of State Capital demanded finding a suitable location for the State Capitol building. The search became a fight between the east and west sides. West-side residents wanted the capitol building on what they called Capitol Hill, the present site of Carroll College. But owner Samuel Hauser wanted ten thousand dollars for the ten-acre site and wouldn't take anything less. East-side residents had reason to favor the current location between Broadway and Sixth Avenue. It was a straight shot down Roberts Street to the Northern Pacific depot. Supporters claimed that the site's higher elevation allowed a better view of the valley, and besides, they claimed, it was ten degrees warmer in winter. Plus, developer Peter Winne offered the land for free with an additional four thousand dollars in donated funds for landscaping. Needless to say, Winne had the better offer and Hauser hung onto his land. Later, Hauser's daughter, Mrs. A. P. Thatcher, held title to the first Capitol Hill and, along with several others, donated a total of fifty acres for the building of Carroll College in 1909.

Capitol Dome

WITH one brief interlude, the copper dome has remained one of the most stunning features of the Montana State Capitol.* That interlude occurred in 1933 during the Depression when a "capitol idea" turned dreadful. The weathered copper needed replacing, but copper was too expensive, and so Secretary of State Sam Mitchell and others proposed painting the dome with aluminum paint. The paint was supposed to brighten the dome's appearance and protect the thin copper sheathing from further wear. Once the dome was painted, it shone like a beacon. Former Helenan Sherman S. Cook recalled, "It was brilliant, all right. In fact, it was indescribably hideous and Helena had to live with that monstrous cooking pot for months." Finally, the Anaconda Copper Mining Company donated the copper, and a crew, put to work with Works Progress Administration funds, undertook the monumental and dangerous job of re-coppering the dome. Secretary of State Mitchell opposed the project, but he was the only one who liked the aluminum paint. Attorney General Raymond Nagle approved the project over Mitchell's objections.

Homestead Teachers

THE homestead boom brought thousands of immigrants and challenged teachers who had few resources in one-room schools. Charles Beardsley, at seventeen, had a college degree and a provisional certificate when he began teaching at Five-Mile School in eastern Montana. He boarded in a student's home for thirty dollars a month. His board was the only money the family earned that entire year. Beardsley wrote: "Bedbugs infested the house. In my bedroom, which was nicely whitewashed, the bed stood in four pans of kerosene to prevent the bedbugs from finding me. I never got a single bite but at night when I was reading, the heat of the kerosene lamp focused on the ceiling and the bedbugs gathered up there for a merry circle dance." The family had bitter ongoing feuds with local relatives. They also kept a pack of hound dogs that bayed all night. They wore shoes only on Sundays, carrying them to church and only putting them on once they were inside. These colorful folk spoke an odd New England dialect and read an archaic kind of music. But they left a permanent impression on the young teacher. Beardsley wrote that the children in this family were very fine, for all their odd behaviors, and they so loved to learn. This rich experience inspired Beardsley's life as an educator, and he enjoyed a long career following his avocation.

Anaconda* versus Helena

THE capital fight between Helena and Anaconda in 1894 pitted Copper King Marcus Daly of Anaconda against Copper King William A. Clark, who backed Helena. It was a very nasty contest fraught with so much bribery and corruption that when the figures were later tallied, the vicious campaign cost more than 3 million dollars. During the campaign, Anacondans portrayed Helenans as a bunch of insufferable snobs. Someone anonymously produced a survey of the Anaconda workingman versus the Helena snob. The survey found more than 2,600 men in Helena who wore silk hats but only 3 in Anaconda. In Helena there were 2 dinner buckets in daily use, but over 4,000 in Anaconda; in Helena there were no men wearing overalls, but over 3,200 in Anaconda; no children in Helena made mud pies, but nearly 2,300 in Anaconda enjoyed playing in the dirt. No men had patches on their trousers in Helena, but 322 had patched knees in Anaconda; 1,600 men in Helena had a patched conscience compared to only 8 in Anaconda; and finally there were 1,300 skeletons in Helena closets, but only 16 in Anaconda. Whose do you suppose they were?

Investors

HELENA, with Copper King William A. Clark's backing, won an expensive, hard-fought race against Marcus Daly and his smelter-town of Anaconda to become Montana's permanent capital. On the heels of this race in 1894, Helena was in its heyday. Even though its population stood only at about thirteen thousand, the wealth and cosmopolitan sophistication visitors to the capital city encountered were deceptive. These belied the town's small population and humble origins. Edmund O'Connell, who was the steward at the far-famed Montana Club,* loved to tell about a prominent club member who invited some easterners out west hoping to secure financial backing on a mining venture. It was after dark when he greeted his guests at the train depot and whisked them to the Montana Club. There he wined and dined them like royalty. When the club closed at two A.M., a waiting carriage conveyed the guests to the Castle, where madam Mollie Byrnes and her ladies entertained them till dawn. The waiting carriage then sped the visitors back to the depot, where they boarded the train for their return to the East. Once back home, an acquaintance asked one of the visitors where he had been. "Helena, Montana," he replied. "How big a place is that?" asked the acquaintance. Thinking back upon his whirlwind adventure in the Queen City, and estimating the population, the traveler replied, "Judging from what I saw, I'd say at least half a million."

The Fern

In 1878, a group of prominent Montanans including W. F. Wheeler, C. W. Cannon, and John Murphy began to investigate the feasibility of steamboat travel between Townsend and Great Falls. After a successful trip in small skiffs from Stubbs' Ferry at Townsend to Fort Benton, they wholeheartedly believed in their enterprise. Finally, in 1887, their steamer, the *Fern,* was ready for her maiden voyage. Built at Twin Bridges, the *Fern* could carry seventy-five tons of freight and one hundred passengers. Investors intended for travelers to leave Helena on the morning train to Townsend. At Stubbs' Ferry, they would board Judge Nicholas Hilger's smaller excursion boat, the *Rose of Helena,* on which they would travel to the Gates of the Mountains. The next day, they would board the *Fern* and complete the journey to Great Falls. Roundtrip from Helena to Great Falls would take four days. But the *Fern* was no match for the treacherous upper Missouri. The *Fern*'s maiden voyage was a nightmare of dredging and towing. After weeks, the *Fern* finally arrived at Great Falls. The *Great Falls Tribune* politely called the trip "successful" and in a sense it was. The *Fern*'s struggle demonstrated for all time the impracticability of navigating that stretch of the muddy Missouri with vessels of her tonnage.

Special Places

*Fort Connah**

ONE of Montana's most important, but nearly forgotten, historical gems is on U.S. Highway 93 at Post Creek in Lake County. This is the site of Fort Connah, a trading post established by the British Hudson's Bay Company in 1846. It was the powerful company's last post built within the boundaries of the United States and represents the British effort to stave off competition from American traders west of the Continental Divide. Fort Connah went unnoticed when the 1846 Oregon Treaty established U.S. ownership of land below the forty-ninth parallel. Angus McDonald took charge of the post in 1847, naming it Fort Connen after a river valley in his native Scotland. The name evolved through Native American usage to Fort Connah. It was an important link between forts on either side of the Rocky Mountains and, besides trading in furs, it was the only source west of the divide for rawhide and hair cordage. Hudson's Bay Company defied the law, operating the post during the twilight of the fur trade era until 1871. The Fort Connah Restoration Society maintains the property, which includes the McDonald family cemetery. The single surviving fort structure, built in 1846 of channeled log according to company specifications, is Montana's oldest building.

Fort Owen*

✴ FORT OWEN near Stevensville witnessed dramatic changes as the Bitterroot Valley emerged from wilderness to settled community. The Jesuit fathers who had established St. Mary's Mission* nearby in 1841 closed their doors in 1850, and John Owen, a former sutler for the U.S. Army, became its new owner. But his fort was not a military site. Owen expanded the mills, cultivated the fields, enlarged the fort, and kept a well-stocked trade room, transforming the former mission into a vibrant trading post. A man of many talents, Owen also served as agent to the Flathead Nation from 1856 to 1862. Owen and his Shoshone wife, Nancy, extended gracious hospitality to Indians, traders, trappers, missionaries, settlers, and travelers. With the 1860s gold rush came a fresh clientele, but the new Mullan Road bypassed Fort Owen, and eventually trading dwindled. Nancy died in 1868. Owen's mental health deteriorated and he became an indigent, committed to St. John's Hospital at Helena. In 1872, the fort was sold at a sheriff's sale. The territory refused to support Owen and deported him. Friends escorted him back East, where he lived another decade with relatives. The state acquired Fort Owen in 1937. The University of Montana's archaeological investigations exposed the fort's walls and foundations. Today, the Stevensville Historical Society continues stabilization and maintenance of this important state monument.

Grant-Kohrs Ranch*

✴ JOHNNY GRANT, founder of the Grant-Kohrs Ranch at Deer Lodge, was a Métis whose mother had been of French and Indian descent. Grant and his wife, Quarra, a Bannock woman, were the first settlers in the Deer Lodge Valley. They acquired horses and cattle in trade from immigrants along the Oregon Trail and, in 1859, they brought two hundred fifty horses and eight hundred cattle into the valley. Soon there was a very ethnically diverse settlement that included Indians, Mexicans, French, and Canadian Métis like Johnny himself. According to pioneer Francis M. Thompson, who was a guest at the ranch, Grant had a wife from every tribe that frequented the Deer Lodge Valley. Grant kept the peace when there was trouble by first determining which tribe was involved. He then brought out his wife and children from that group, hiding other family members. While this is probably an exaggeration, by 1863 Grant did have eleven children with four different Indian women. In 1892, gold discoveries attracted miners and white settlers. Grant's ranch was vandalized, his best barn burned, and the revenue officer harassed him. The days when neighbors were tolerant of other cultures and interracial marriages came to an end. Grant sold his ranch to Conrad Kohrs and in 1867 left Montana and returned to Canada.

*Heikkila-Mattila Homestead**

Finnish immigrant Gust Heikkila homesteaded along the Little Belt Creek coulee in 1902. Soon other Finnish settlers homesteaded the area, calling it Korpivaara, meaning "dangerous wilderness," for its remote wooded surroundings. Here the Heikkilas raised eleven children, expanded their holdings, and were among the first to shift from farming to ranching. The skills of Gust and local Finnish builders Victor Mattila and Matt Maki reveal an outstanding folk vernacular building style that transferred the Finnish farmstead to a New World setting. The men showcased their traditional skills, building a sauna, residence, and other structures using Old World tools like the broadaxe and awl. The result is a classic Finnish farm with log buildings around an open courtyard. In 1938, the sons of Victor Mattila, who helped build the homestead, bought the property from the Heikkalas. The brothers, trained in woodworking by carpenter Matt Maki, expanded some of the buildings and also built new ones. The result is American in design but

Finnish in construction. The 1938 barn, in particular, represents a masterful blending of the two cultures by second-generation Finnish builders. This unusual homestead, listed on the National Register of Historic Places, is one interesting example of building by Montana's diverse European homesteaders.

Scherlie Homestead*

THE Enlarged Homestead Act of 1909 lured many home-steaders to Montana and to an area in Blaine County called the Big Flat. One of these was thirty-two-year-old Anna Scherlie, who arrived in 1913 to file a claim near her brother's place. Anna was one of many women homesteaders who worked Montana claims. In fact, in the four surrounding townships, women made up about one-fourth of the total homestead applicants. By 1916, Anna had forty acres planted in wheat, oats, and flax. Isolation on the Big Flat led many settlers to winter elsewhere, and Anna followed suit. Legend has it that she went to St. Paul to work for the family of railroad magnate James J. Hill. Over the decades, Anna made few changes to her small wood-frame shack, adding only a vestibule to use as a summer kitchen and laundry. Droughts, depression, and two world wars passed. Anna's neighbors built modern homes, but she insisted that she was too old for modern conveniences. Anna died in 1973, leaving an estate of more than one hundred thousand dollars to eighteen nieces and nephews. Her ashes were scattered beneath a lilac bush on the property. Leon and Nellie Cederburg purchased the homestead, but rather than return it to cropland, the Cederburgs maintain Anna's home exactly as she left it.

Crail Ranch*

THE Spanish Peaks, the Madison Range, and the Gallatin Canyon provided a magnificent backdrop for Augustus Frank

Crail's ranch. In 1902, Crail carved 960 acres out of three home-steads, school lands, and railroad property. He, his wife, and three children settled in a small log cabin while they built the main house using a water-powered sawmill. They also milled lumber to sell. Crail grew a special kind of wheat he developed and raised sheep. By 1934, the Crails' success allowed them to begin raising cattle. Many local ranchers who weathered the Great Depression turned to dude ranching, but the Crails continued to farm and run cattle until 1950. For fifty years, the ranch structures were the only evidence of human habitation in this meadow valley. Today, the house and cabin are the sole survivors of the once-sprawling complex. The sturdy main residence, built with care and skill in 1905, is of hand-hewn logs chinked with mortar. The marks of the ax used to flatten the dove-tailed logs are plainly visible. The two dwellings, now nestled among modern residences, are a rare monument to early home-steading and a poignant reminder of this bygone era in the modern ski-destination resort known today as Big Sky.

Stearns Hall*

THE small settlement of Stearns near Wolf Creek emerged in the early 1890s as homesteaders filed claims between Wolf Creek and Augusta. By 1900, Stearns boasted a school and post office. The Enlarged Homestead Act of 1909 brought new arrivals, and in 1910, Stearns had need of a community hall. Local members of the Modern Woodmen of America coordinated the construction. Using lumber milled of logs from the south fork of the Dearborn River, local builders experienced in barn raising designed the spacious hall. A St. Patrick's Day dance christened the two-story hall in 1911. The second floor was removed in 1912 to allow for basketball games, and the facility became the center of social activity. Drought and depression ended the homestead boom, and the population of

Stearns dwindled after 1921. The automobile simplified travel to larger towns, and the hall was even less frequently used for community activities. In the 1940s, it served as a dining room and dormitory for construction crews working on Highway 200 over Rogers Pass. While other reminders of Stearns have fallen victim to time, you can still see Stearns Hall. It's a lonely representative of one community that rose and fell with America's last homestead boom.

Sedman House

ONE of Montana's best-kept secrets is the Sedman House, a beautifully furnished territorial period home in Nevada City, now under state ownership and maintained by the Montana Heritage Commission. It originally stood in nearby Junction City, where it was one of the first large homes built in the region in 1873. Its builder, Madison County rancher and territorial legislator Oscar Sedman, met an unfortunate end. In 1881, during the legislative session in Helena, he suddenly took ill and died of "black measles," the tick-borne disease we know today as Rocky Mountain spotted fever. Sedman was the first Montana legislator to die during a session. He left a wife and four small children. His colleagues paid him tribute by draping his official chair in black crepe, turning it backward to face the wall. After Oscar's death, two of the Sedmans' four children died. Mrs. Sedman remarried and moved to Missoula. The Sedmans' lovely home later became the Junction Hotel. After that, it served as a stable. Charles Bovey disassembled the badly deteriorated building and moved it a mile and a half to Nevada City, where he put it back together. The home today is a focal point. The period furnishings include the desk of vigilante prosecutor Wilbur Fisk Sanders and Colonel Charles Broadwater's personal gold-trimmed bathtub from his private suite at the far-famed Broadwater Hotel. A visit to the Sedman House in Nevada City is well worth it.

Sieben Ranch

THE Sieben Ranch encompasses a vast 115,000 acres in Lewis and Clark County. It has a rich archaeological history that includes fragments of the roads that brought miners to Montana's goldfields. Trader Malcolm Clarke was the first to settle on a knoll overlooking Prickly Pear Creek in 1864 where he ran a stage stop. Clarke, embittered over his expulsion from West Point because of an altercation with a fellow student, had come west with the American Fur Company in 1841. The itinerant trader finally settled down on his ranch to raise horses and cattle. A dispute with Clarke's Blackfeet in-laws and trouble in Fort Benton between whites and Blackfeet led to his murder at the ranch in 1869. Clarke's family buried him on a gentle rise north of the house. Pioneer rancher James Fergus added the Clarke ranch to his large holdings in 1875. General William T. Sherman, an overnight guest at the Fergus house in 1877, stumbled upon Clarke's grave. He was saddened to discover Clarke's fate. The two had been classmates at West Point, and Sherman had long wondered what became of the promising young cadet. Henry Sieben purchased the ranch in 1897, and it remains in the Sieben-Baucus family today, still a working sheep ranch with a legacy its owners treasure.

Glendive

AUTHOR Marian T. Place wrote that the town of Glendive was born "astraddle the tracks with its back to the river and its face toward the soaring badlands." It is a fitting portrayal. This tenacious community began as a steamboat landing on the Yellowstone River and took root as a railroad center in the middle of prime livestock country. When the Northern Pacific reached Glendive in 1881, its first cars transported buffalo hides and bones back to the "states" and river travel became a thing of the past. Soon, countless head of cattle were unloaded at Glendive, filling Montana's empty prairies. Sheep and cattle ranchers enthusiastically promoted the region's grazing lands, and the town's business opportunities grew when it was designated the county seat. The *Glendive Times* encouraged newcomers, even promising single women "a 'right smart' chance to catch on to husbands." Town boosters described Glendive's setting as a "natural amphitheater, surrounded by rugged hills." But it's interesting that town boosters very carefully avoided the term *badlands*. The colorful layers of sediment tourists so enjoy today in nearby Makoshika State Park, sometimes described as "hell cooked over," were then considered a serious drawback to settlement.

Deer Lodge Woman's Club*

WOMEN'S suffrage was at the political forefront when Edward Gardner Lewis, a promoter and publisher of women's magazines, founded the American Women's League in 1908. Lewis promoted American womanhood through his magazines and founded a correspondence school called the People's University. Chapter houses across the country served as University branches. Women earned membership in the League by selling subscriptions to Lewis's magazines. In exchange, the League constructed thirty-nine local chapter houses in sixteen states. There were two in Montana, one at Avon and one at Deer Lodge. Deer Lodge women collected the required subscriptions for their clubhouse, and C. D. Terret donated land. Construction had just begun when financial reversals sent Lewis into bankruptcy. Alma Bielenberg Higgins, a founder of the Deer Lodge League, persuaded her father, Nicholas Bielenberg, to purchase the mortgage. He donated the house to the women of Deer Lodge in memory of his daughter, Augusta, who died in 1901. The Deer Lodge Woman's Club still maintains the clubhouse at 802 Missouri Avenue. The charming bungalow has always served as a women's cultural, literary, and social center.

Bielenberg House*

PIONEER stockman, financier, and mining investor Nick Bielenberg came to Montana via Fort Benton in 1865. He, his brothers John and Charles, and half-brother Conrad Kohrs were all butchers by trade. They eventually settled in Deer Lodge. The brothers were all involved in large-scale cattle operations. While Conrad Kohrs of the Grant-Kohrs Ranch* is the best known of the brothers, Nick Bielenberg made his own reputation establishing a wholesale meat business in Butte. It became famous throughout the Northwest for pioneering cold storage methods. Prominent in the Deer Lodge community, Bielenberg was a charter member of the Montana Stockgrowers Association, brought some of the first livestock into the Deer Lodge Valley, and pioneered Montana's sheep industry. Bielenberg built a stunning bungalow-style home in Deer Lodge in 1910. Its brick came by rail from Milwaukee, Wisconsin, and a contractor brought in from St. Paul, Minnesota, supervised the masons and carpenters. Oak-framed doorways and original brass fixtures grace the interior, while Bielenberg's trophies in a glassed-in gable added a personal footnote. The Bielenbergs entertained such famous Montanans as artist Edgar S. Paxson, Jeannette Rankin, and Gary Cooper.

Bluestone House*

HELENANS have all heard the story about how architect James Stranahan built the Bluestone House for his bride and died before they could move in. But the true story is much more interesting than that. Stranahan was the architect, but title records show that the house was built as a residence for Lillie McGraw, one of Helena's three wealthy proprietor madams. Stranahan did die during construction of the house in 1889, and Lillie suffered financial setbacks.

There was a lien on the property, and it reverted to Stranahan's wife, Leona. She immediately sold the unfinished house to J. S. M. Neill, who sold it to artist Ralph DeCamp. The house continued to change hands until 1924 when James McIntosh, whose backyard adjoined the Bluestone House, became its long-term owner. Relatives of the McIntoshes did live in the house in the early 1930s, but they have been its only occupants. The home suffered extensive earthquake damage in 1935. Proximity to the red light district that once sprawled below it and its fortress-like appearance led to its mistaken identity as the Castle, a high-class brothel that operated nearby. Chet Huntley perpetuated this myth in the centennial film *Last Chance Gulch*. Restored during urban renewal, the house later served as a restaurant and is now a law office.

Lavina

LAVINA, forty miles north of Billings, is a tiny community with a large history. "Old" Lavina grew along the Musselshell River at the endpoint of the annual livestock roundups. By the spring of 1882, Thomas C. Power knew the Northern Pacific would soon reach Billings, and he built a stage line linking Lavina and Fort Benton. A stage stop and saloon awaited travelers at Lavina. The settlement became a hub for freighters and travelers. As the Milwaukee Road Company built its line across Montana, officials considered old Lavina as a depot, but it sat too near the river. So company vice president John Q. Adams selected a new townsite a mile downstream and relocated Lavina there. The first train steamed into town in 1908. The Adams Hotel,* named for John Q. Adams, welcomed travelers. First-class services included twenty-one rooms, steam heat, gas lighting, imported wines and fine meals, linen sheets, and hot baths. The Adams Hotel became a regional social center. But with the exodus of disappointed homesteaders in the

1920s, the hotel closed. The American Lutheran Church used the bar as a chapel through the 1970s. Today, the old hotel's private owner is working to restore its former glory.

Adair Mercantile*

REMOTE wilderness where a man could live by his own rules drew Bill Adair to northwestern Montana in 1904. He built a log mercantile on the east side of the North Fork of the Flathead River, supplying goods to the few settlers in the sparsely populated area. When the designation of Glacier National Park in 1910 eliminated homesteading on his side of the river, Adair saw that his future lay across the river where homesteaders continued to settle. Choosing a spot with exceptional fishing nearby, Adair filed a land claim in 1912 and built a cabin and a false-fronted mercantile. On twenty-two acres, Adair grew hay, potatoes, timothy grass, and garden vegetables. From 1913 to 1920, Adair's was the only general store in the North Fork region and a favorite spot for social events. By 1922, more than 150 homesteads dotted the fifty-mile stretch of valley bottom, but the area never became heavily populated. Even today, the Polebridge Mercantile continues to serve its few North Fork residents and welcome visitors, while the splendid, unspoiled environment remains one of Montana's best-kept secrets.

B Street Brothels

EVERY Montana town had its red light district, and remnants of these places survive in many communities. Buildings and houses have usually been adapted for other uses and their histories forgotten. One exception is the railroad town of Livingston's quaint little B Street Historic District,* once a thriving neighborhood that catered to railroaders. At one time there were nine houses. Five of them on the street's east side survive. Built between 1896 and

1904, these unusual little cottages feature gables and porches that resemble those of larger homes. Identical in composition, they have front porches with thin columns and small attic windows. Each had two separate front doors, a brick chimney on each half, and three small rooms, called "cribs," on each side. There was also a small waiting area just inside each front door. Mid-range brothels like these often housed cribs enclosed within the house and were built without kitchens and bathrooms. These types of establishments were meant to look like real homes, but they had no conveniences. They gave patrons—in Livingston, mostly traveling railroad men— the impression of a "home away from home," but in reality offered few creature comforts. Livingston's B Street District operated until it closed in 1948. Four of the cottages, resembling tiny wooden temples, retain good architectural integrity. Homeowners in one of the houses removed the partitions and added a loft. Wanting others to appreciate their home's interesting history, they also preserved a patch in the floor, added during the historic period, to cover a hole worn by an iron bedstead.

Matt's Place*

BUTTE entrepreneur Matt Korn opened a tiny restaurant in 1930 featuring a drive-in window, an idea he imported from southern California. Matt's Place was likely Montana's first drive-in. He never advertised, but built his reputation on good food. Korn soon expanded the drive-in to include curb service. In 1936, high school student Mabel Waddell, who used to visit Korn's tiny drive-in window as a child, joined the staff of seven carhops. Korn mistakenly had "Mae" embroidered on her uniform, prompting Mabel to change her name. Mae continued to work at Matt's Place, and in 1943, she and her new husband, Louis Lawrence, bought the drive-in. They spent their honeymoon waiting on customers. Over the next half century, more than twenty-eight family members have worked for Mae at the drive-in. The menu hasn't changed since the 1930s, and Matt's Place has won national acclaim for its homemade burgers and shakes, vintage equipment, and period furnishings. One out-of-stater summed it up, "Now I know it's not the mountains and lakes that make Montana special," he wrote, "it's Matt's Place!" Be sure to check it out when you're in Butte.

Butte Speakeasy

JAMES PRATT, owner of the longtime Red Boot and Shoe Company in Butte, built his Rookwood Hotel* in the Mining City for thirty thousand dollars in 1912. Unusual green tile decorates the building, and a beautiful marble entry leads into the forty-five-room hotel. Inside, a wrought-iron staircase with marble treads took guests down to the elegant hotel lobby. The hotel later became a rooming house. During Prohibition in the late 1910s and 1920s, the thirty working-class lodgers likely enjoyed a secret. During a recent cleanup of the building, workers discovered a speakeasy tucked beneath the sidewalk. Untouched for decades, the hidden entry and two-way mirror confirm the clandestine use. Butte was rumored to have had more than one hundred illegal underground drinking places during Prohibition. Elaborate columns with elegant carved griffins, thick terrazzo flooring, dark hardwood, marble trim, and a colorful stained-glass skylight make this certainly one of the most beautiful speakeasies west of Chicago. You can experience the Rookwood Speakeasy, a wonderful piece of Butte's once-spirited underground, through Old Butte Historical Adventures.

Daniels County Courthouse*

SCOBEY, the seat of Daniels County, has Montana's most unusual courthouse. It is a stunning false-fronted building, painted a crisp white. But it has a rather shady past. The building has been enlarged and remodeled inside. What was once a spacious hotel lobby is now divided into county offices. But the courthouse began as a hotel, built sometime before 1913 when the town of Scobey relocated from its original site along the Poplar River flats. This hotel had several owners, but during most of the teens, One-Eyed Molly Wakefield owned the building. Molly was a rough character who earned her nickname because she was blind in one eye. A long scar ran across it, hinting at some violent episode in her mysterious past. She came on the train from Kansas City with her four sons, all her belongings, and money in her pockets. Molly bought real estate, including the hotel. She and her sons kept pit bulls for fighting staked between her hotel and the Tallman Hotel next door. There was gambling in Molly's hotel, as there was in Scobey's other hotels, but women were the main attraction. The hotel had no indoor bathroom facilities, although the first-floor rooms for entertaining were handily equipped with sinks. A large sleeping room upstairs accommodated legitimate overnight guests. In 1917, federal officials closed red light districts across the nation. One-Eyed Molly disappeared, and her hotel sat empty. When Scobey became the county seat in 1920, officials had no reservations about taking over the old hotel. Even today, some of the county offices retain telltale sinks. It is Montana's only brothel-turned-courthouse.

Goosetown*

THOUSANDS of immigrants came to work for Marcus Daly in Anaconda, and most settled in Goosetown, a neighborhood that nestles under the shadow of the Great Stack. Workers' cottages, boarding houses, and homes on narrow lots with bachelor cabins at the rear, rented for a little extra income, are common. Small businesses like saloons and groceries as well as the 1905 Washoe Brewery illustrate the private commerce that Daly allowed to flourish alongside smelter-related enterprises. Many women lost their husbands to the dangerous work, and widows in Goosetown usually maintained their families by operating small businesses from their homes. Ethnic churches included Austrian Roman Catholic, Free Swedish Mission, Norwegian Evangelical Lutheran, and Serbian Orthodox, hinting at ethnically oriented organizations that offered camaraderie and comfort far from home. Two theories explain the origins of the name *Goosetown*. One attributes it to the practice of saloons keeping turkeys and geese to raffle off at Thanksgiving. Another theory holds that the neighborhood's initial freshwater system consisted of a water tap at the end of a gooseneck pipe in each residential yard. Choose the theory you like best!

Rural Schools

Montana's school system has come a long way. In 1880, the average person went to school for about four years. By 1900, the number had risen to five. Many early teachers had only an eighth grade education, but the Normal School at Dillon began turning out trained teachers in the late 1890s. In Montana's early rural schools, the youngest students started in the smallest seats and progressed to larger desks along the rows or around the room. When they got to the other side of the room or the end of the line, they usually quit and went to work. Sometimes schools were held in strange places. One classroom was located in a cow pasture. The building had no foundation, but was set upon large rocks. Every time the cows rubbed against it, the whole school would rock back and forth. The outhouse was made of apple crates and boards, and every time there was a slight wind, it blew over. Rural teachers boarded with families or lived in one-room teacherages attached to their schools. One teacher in northern Toole County arrived to replace someone who had quit in the middle of the term. One of the local farmers met her train at Shelby in a bobsled, took her to buy supplies, and dropped her off at the teacherage. A storm came up, and when the farmer could finally check on her, he found her frozen to death under piles of blankets and clothing. In buying her supplies, she neglected to buy matches.

One-Room Schools

GALLATIN COUNTY, one of the original nine counties established in 1865 during territorial days, was the first area in Montana settled for extensive farming. The homesteaders who followed the miners in the late 1860s established schools in private homes or one-room cabins. Tiny schoolhouses dotted the countryside, often no more than five miles apart. Because of cold weather, the school year was only four months long. Frame schoolhouses began to replace log cabins. These were usually one room with a central door and an open front porch—an essential feature designed to make young children feel at home. Styles changed. In 1919, one study recommended that classroom windows be on one side only. Officials believed that this would prevent eye strain caused by cross lighting. Vestibules were often added as protection against harsh weather. These changes became the norm in the 1920s. There are sixteen one-room schools remaining in Gallatin County that document these and other environmental and cultural changes in rural schools spanning the time period from territorial days to 1934.

DeBorgia Schoolhouse*

REMNANTS of Indian trails, the Mullan Road, the Milwaukee and Northern Pacific Railroads, and old U.S. Highway 10 lie scattered across a narrow mountain corridor at the west end of Mineral County. There in 1908, the DeBorgia schoolhouse was built to serve local children. Two years later, in 1910, DeBorgia and the neighboring settlements of Haugan and Saltese fell victim to a catastrophic forest fire. The DeBorgia school was the only building left unscathed after the cataclysmic event. The school went on to serve several generations of students from grades one through eight. During the teens, Neil Stoughton went through all eight grades at the school. Each year he was the only student in his class, a fact recorded in *Ripley's Believe It or Not*. Although the school closed in 1956, the simple clapboard building with its wooded lawn and flagpole continued to serve as a community gathering place. In 1969, a small group of spirited ladies assumed responsibility for maintenance and preservation of the building. With their dedication and the support of other local groups, this historic treasure has continued to serve the tiny West End communities of Mineral County.

Medicine in the Making

Gold Rush Doctors

THE lure of gold drew Dr. Jerome S. Glick to Bannack in 1862, but soon his skills earned him a fine reputation as a bone surgeon. One of his most highly acclaimed operations was performed at gunpoint on Bannack's infamous sheriff, Henry Plummer, who had taken a well-aimed bullet in his shooting arm. In 1865, Dr. Glick formed a partnership with Dr. Ira Maupin. The two friends often answered calls together, traveling long distances and operating under the worst possible conditions. Called to a nearby mining camp one freezing January night, they found three critically wounded gunshot victims lying in the snow. Working by candlelight in a crude cabin, the doctors saved two of the men. Dr. Glick was highly skilled at setting broken bones and saving limbs, but he also performed many skillful amputations. The doctor amputated the arm of a three-year-old boy within the space of one minute with no anesthetic, and the child apparently felt no pain. Dr. Maupin and Dr. Glick often drove miles to treat indigent patients. On the way home from such a trip in 1873, Dr. Maupin's horse threw him and he died the following day; his patient died three days later. Dr. Glick carried on the practice alone. He wore his hair very long and wore a large black hat. He rode a spirited white horse. Mexican tappederos on his stirrups always attracted attention. After his partner's death, Dr. Glick practiced alone until his death in 1880. Mary Ronan, whose husband was the Flathead Indian agent, wrote about how everyone loved Dr. Glick. She knew him well, and he delivered several of her eight children. Dr. Glick later suffered from dementia. "The pathos of his condition," Ronan wrote, "was intensely poignant to those of us who had known him in his vigorous days of supreme service."

Caroline McGill

DR. CAROLINE MCGILL came to Butte in 1911 to work at the Murray Hospital, returned to Johns Hopkins to complete her medical degree, and turned down an offer to stay at Johns Hopkins to return to Butte in 1914. She practiced there until she retired in 1956. Dr. McGill was a highly skilled physician, but she was also a friend to her patients through Butte's ugly labor management strife, fires, explosions, and accidents that were common in the mining town. She made house calls to the crudest of miner's shacks where she ministered to families under primitive conditions. She once said, "I made up my mind that I would never offend one of these good women by seeming to notice that their standards of sanitation were not mine. I couldn't abide the habit of some of my colleagues of dusting off a chair with a clean handkerchief before daring to sit on it." Dr. McGill was a familiar figure in saloons, where stabbings, gunshot wounds, fractures, and concussions tested her skills. She frequently visited the women of Butte's sprawling red light district, calling equally at low-rent cribs and high-class parlor houses. Small, attractive, and full of energy, Dr. McGill was a cut above the rest.

Challenge at Elkhorn

GUNSHOT wounds, childbirth, mining accidents, frostbite, spotted fever, and dreaded epidemics created a battleground for courageous doctors who honed their skills on the Montana frontier. Elkhorn was one such challenge for Dr. William H. Dudley, who came west in 1885. Employed at Elkhorn, Dr. Dudley wrote to his sweetheart back in Connecticut, and she made the long journey west alone. Dr. Dudley met her train in Butte, and the wedding took place immediately. The newlyweds then traveled by sleigh to Elkhorn. Some 2,500 people lived in close proximity to each other in the silver camp, and they were especially vulnerable to communicable diseases. Lack of an adequate water supply left Elkhorn residents at high risk. Dr. Dudley and his colleague reached the limits of their skills during 1888 and 1889 when diphtheria, likely spread via bacteria-contaminated water, struck the community. The graves of those who succumbed to this epidemic dot Elkhorn's hillside cemetery. The Dudleys returned to New York in 1889 expecting the birth of their second child, but they left their firstborn son, a victim of the epidemic, buried on the wooded slope overlooking Elkhorn.

Maria Dean

THE medical facility adjacent to St. Peter's Hospital in Helena bears the name of a woman whose contributions to the early community were significant. Educated at the Boston University School of Medicine, Maria Dean studied further in Germany in the early 1880s. She experienced the usual contempt for professional women and was first given the most menial jobs and hopeless cases. Eventually her diligence paid off, and she won the highest commendations of her professors and fellow male students. Dr. Dean came to Helena in the mid-1880s, where she became one of the first women physicians in the territory. She was an excellent buggy driver, and her high-spirited team was a familiar sight along the bumpy backroads of Lewis and Clark County. In 1885, Dr. Dean was chairman of the Board of Health during a diphtheria epidemic. She was the first to implement quarantine, placing warning flags at homes where the disease was present. Dr. Dean was the first woman to practice at St. Peter's Hospital, served as chairman of the Helena Board of Education, and helped establish the Helena YWCA and Mountain View School for Girls. She died in 1919. Her tombstone inscription appropriately reads, "Our Beloved Physician."

Rocky Mountain Fever

THE Montana State Board of Health was created in 1901. At its first meeting, Montana's labor commissioner addressed the board on behalf of the lumber industry on the subject of spotted fever. Cases had been documented since 1873 in the Bitterroot Valley. Known as "black measles" for its characteristic blue-black rash, the disease was troubling because of its mysterious origin and lack of treatment. Montana cases, especially in the Bitterroot Valley, were almost always fatal. Nineteenth-century theories about its cause were many. Most, including doctors, believed it came from drinking melted snow. Others thought the sawdust piles at Marcus Daly's Hamilton lumber mill were to blame, and still others thought the cause was the spring winds blowing over decaying vegetation. As the Bitterroot Valley stood on the brink of the apple boom in the early 1900s, there were economic reasons to pursue the study of spotted fever. No one wanted to settle on land and live in constant fear of this disease. Governor Edwin Norris in 1912 advised that any publicity about spotted fever would adversely affect settlement in the Bitterroot Valley. It was not until State Senator and Mrs. Tyler Worden of Lolo both died of spotted fever in 1921 that Montana received national publicity about the disease. Although a handful of researchers in Montana died of spotted fever, their work led to the discovery of ticks as the cause and the development of a vaccine. In the 1920s, Hamilton became the site of the Rocky Mountain Laboratory.* There, researchers bred infected ticks by the millions for the production of a vaccine that virtually eradicated the disease.

Spanish Flu

In 1918, the nation faced a shortage of doctors and nurses because of World War I. This was especially true of Montana, where fully 10 percent of the male population served in the military. The homestead boom in 1909 boosted Montana's population, but drought and depression in the teens caused many to leave the state. Military quotas based on the 1910 census caused a disproportionate number of men to be drafted into service. Shortages were thus even more acute in Montana. Spanish influenza swept the nation, drastically compounding these shortages. The terrifying onset of Spanish flu created a situation similar to concerns in the early twenty-first century with the war raging in the Near East, threats of bird flu, and other global health concerns. The first cases of Spanish influenza hit Montana in October 1918, and the illness spread so rapidly and was so deadly that when Armistice was declared in November, public celebrations were forbidden. Many Montana communities formed chapters of the Red Cross as flu found its way to every corner of the state. By the next spring, more than 26,000 Montanans had suffered from the flu; 2,436 died, more than three times the state's nine hundred World War I casualties. Author Alfred Crosby, in his book *America's Forgotten Pandemic: The Influenza of 1918,* said that there was no medicine to fight the flu. It was tender loving care, warm food, and warm blankets that kept patients alive until the disease ran its course. That, he says, was the real miracle drug of 1918.

A Legacy of War

O. G. Willett was an army veteran, a state senator, and the person who suggested the name for Mineral County. He was also the victim of a dreaded disease. Willett had suffered undiagnosed bouts of illness, but while he was serving in the legislature in 1917, the Mayo Clinic finally determined the cause. Willett had leprosy. He had become infected while serving his country in the Philippines in 1902. The State of Montana at this time had rules and regulations in place for the isolation and quarantine of lepers, since leprosy was believed to be a fatal and highly contagious disease. Willett and his wife were placed under quarantine in a small cottage in rural Mineral County near Alberton and cared for at county expense. In 1927, a legislative act committed Willett—who had refused medical treatment—to the federal leprosarium at Carville, Louisiana. Although local residents had been supportive of the Willetts, arsonists wasted little time after their departure for Louisiana and burned their house down. Doctors at Carville were hopeful. Willett was not disfigured, but the disease was far advanced. Despite treatment, he died in 1928. Today, Carville, Louisiana, is home to the National Hansen's Disease Museum. Although the museum was undamaged by Hurricaine Katrina, services there were disrupted while it served as the identification center for 910 victims of the storm.

Epidemics

As in any other place where people lived in close proximity to their neighbors and did not understand how diseases spread, Montana's settlements experienced epidemics. Typhoid and cholera from contaminated water posed a real threat to miners and early settlers while diphtheria, whooping cough, and measles struck children in particular. Yet, as Dr. Jacob J. Leiser wrote in 1881, Montana was actually a healthy territory. He partly attributed its low death rate to the dry climate: "A carcass in the street instead of decomposing," he wrote, " . . . literally dries up, scarcely tainting the air at all." An early proponent of public health and a well-educated physician, Dr. Leiser explained that in 1880, Helena had only three so-called epidemics. The first two, measles and whooping cough, claimed only two lives each. The last and most severe was diphtheria, which took a dozen victims. Helena at that time had about four thousand residents. Dr. Leiser suggested that even two lives lost could be considered an epidemic; five lives lost would be a serious plague. So, in the mid-1860s when seven people died between June 1865 and June 1866 on the Hangman's Tree, it seems fairly obvious that death by hanging was an epidemic.

Evolution of Professional Nursing

FROM early in its history, Montana boasted both Catholic and Protestant teaching hospitals. However, the Montana Deaconess Hospital in Great Falls ushered in a national trend to professionalize nurses' training programs. Chicago-trained deaconess Augusta Ariss founded the school in 1902 and was its superintendent for thirty-three years. The first students served as apprentices, learning firsthand. They also scrubbed floors, laundered bedding, fired the furnace, and prepared patients' meals. Miss Ariss modeled the school after Johns Hopkins in Baltimore and St. Luke's in New York City, following the principles set forth by Florence Nightingale. Students administered medication such as aspirin, codeine, Novocain, and digitalis. Treatments included boric acid and saline solutions for bladder, eye, ear, and nasal irrigations. Students learned that cold baths for typhoid and other diseases brought down fever, hot turpentine stupes relieved abdominal swelling, and flaxseed and mustard plasters reduced inflammation. They used no intravenous therapies. Then in the later 1910s and 1920s, new discoveries like X-rays and radium, oxygen tents, gas anesthesia, the use of insulin for treating diabetes, and advancements in orthopedics revolutionized medicine. The school offered modern, cutting-edge training. In 1937, under Superintendent Pearl Sherrick, the Montana Deaconess School of Nursing affiliated with Montana State College at Bozeman. It became Montana's first fully accredited nursing school.

Missions, Churches, and Clergy

Sisters of Charity

To nurse the sick, teach children, and care for orphans was the threefold mission of the Sisters of Charity of Leavenworth, Kansas. Established in 1858, the sisters came to Montana in 1869 indirectly because of pioneer newspaperman Peter Ronan. In 1862, Ronan was editor of a small newspaper in Leavenworth. It was the only Democratic newspaper in Kansas at the time. As Civil War politics divided Kansas, the government confiscated Ronan's printing press for his partisan articles. He landed in the jail at Fort Leavenworth. Mother Mary Vincent of the Sisters of Charity visited the prisoners at the fort, bringing them meals and supplying them with clean clothing. She and Ronan became good friends. Later, in the mining camp at Last Chance, when Catholic priests lamented the lack of Catholic education for Montana's youth, Ronan suggested they write to the sisters at Leavenworth. Five nuns and a lay teacher arrived to establish the first Catholic institutions in Montana. Mother Mary Vincent soon joined them. They were the first of many Sisters of Charity who came to Montana. The Catholic sisters fulfilled their mission, establishing the first Catholic boarding school, hospital, and orphanage at Helena. Like the opening of a flower, these institutions paved the way for many others that bloomed all over Montana.

St. Mary's Mission*

✸ THE Salish people of the Bitterroot Valley learned of the "Black Robes" from Jesuit-educated Iroquois. The Salish sent four delegations to St. Louis through dangerous enemy territory, requesting that the Catholic bishop send Jesuit priests to teach them about Christianity. Father Pierre Jean DeSmet arrived in the Bitterroot Valley in 1841 to found Montana's first permanent settlement and the first Catholic mission in the Northwest. The Jesuits at St. Mary's were the first whites to practice agriculture in Montana and instituted many other firsts. The mission closed in 1850, but the seeds, both physical and spiritual, that the Jesuits planted remained viable until the priests returned to reestablish the mission in 1866. Until 1891 when the U.S. government forced the Salish to leave their farms and the graves of their ancestors for the Jocko Valley on the Flathead Reservation, the Jesuits provided financial support, medical services, and spiritual guidance to both the Salish and white settlers. The closing of the mission and the exodus of the Salish is one of the most painful episodes in western history. The untended mission fell into disrepair. Twenty years later, the creation of St. Mary's parish saw the mission in use again. Today, the historic chapel and mission complex serve as a classroom that helps teach hard lessons of history. Salish descendants return to the mission annually to share their stories, keeping the memories of their Bitterroot homeland alive for new generations of schoolchildren.

Father Anthony Ravalli

✸ DURING the 1840s, the first Catholic missionaries came into Montana, settling in the Bitterroot Valley at St. Mary's Mission.* Among the three founding Jesuit priests was Father Anthony Ravalli, the first trained doctor to make Montana his field of medical service. He studied at the University of Padua in Italy and was a man of many talents—a gifted artist, chemist, carpenter, pharmacist, as well as doctor. Father Ravalli traveled widely among the native tribes, especially the Salish, and vaccinated them against the dreaded smallpox. He built Montana's first flour mill, bringing millstones with him from Europe. This gave the native people of the Bitterroot Valley a more digestible food than the boiled wheat grains they were previously used to. He built the first still in Montana, which he used to transform the camas root, a staple of the Salish people, into alcohol for medicinal uses. He standardized Indian remedies and dosages and preserved the medicines in alcohol he made with the first still. Beloved by both Indians and whites, Father Ravalli is buried in the mission cemetery. Because of his contributions, Ravalli County bears his name. In 2005, Father Ravalli received a place in the Gallery of Outstanding Montanans at the State Capitol.

Brother Van

CIRCUIT riding Methodist ministers, "the Lord's Horsemen," arrived in Montana in the 1870s to establish congregations among the territory's early population. Most beloved among them was William Wesley Van Orsdel—known as "Brother Van"—who arrived in Fort Benton on the steamboat *Far West* in 1872. On horseback, by wagon, by rail, and finally by automobile, Brother Van ministered to a far-flung population. In the early days, Brother Van held prayer meetings in stores, barns, one-room cabins, and even saloons across the state. He established more than one hundred churches, six hospitals, a college, and a boarding school. Brother Van never married and spent his time traveling. Legend has it that saloonkeepers gave him a thousand dollars to build himself a home, but he put the money toward building a nurses' residence at the Great Falls Deaconess Hospital. Artist Charlie Russell depicted Brother Van in a painting titled *Shooting the Lead Buffalo*. It depicts a real incident, showing Brother Van at the head of the herd, brandishing a rifle with his coattails flying. It's an unusual portrayal of a man of God, but it reveals Brother Van's ability to fit in almost anywhere. Brother Van served Montana Methodists for forty-five years. When he died in 1919, flags across the state flew at half-staff and the children of the school he founded—whom he loved above all else—sang at his funeral.

St. Ignatius*

JESUITS founded St. Ignatius Mission on the Flathead Reservation in 1854 after the abandonment of St. Mary's Mission in the Bitterroot Valley. From 1875 to 1900, the mission had a shop with a printing press that produced *Narratives from the Holy Scripture* in the Kalispell language and a Kalispell dictionary. A lumber mill, an agricultural and industrial school for boys, a boarding school for girls, and the mission church once sprawled across the landscape on the Flathead Reservation. Church officials laid the cornerstone of the present mission church in 1891. The quaint little church has a surprising treasure. Step inside and be amazed. Its walls and ceilings have sixty-one original paintings done by Brother Joseph Carignano, an Italian Jesuit who was the longtime cook and handyman at the mission. Although he had no formal art training, Brother Carignano painted the interior with murals of scenes from the Old and New Testaments and portraits of some of the saints. He did this magnificent work all in the little spare time he had from his many duties at the mission. His paintings are so astonishing that they have been described as miraculous.

Methodist Deaconesses

THE Deaconess Movement arose from within the Methodist, Lutheran, Episcopal, and other Protestant denominations. It sought to incorporate professional women in ministerial duties.

The Chicago Training School was the center of the movement and prepared its deaconesses to serve as missionary nurses, teachers, and social workers. Unlike Catholic sisters, deaconesses took no perpetual vows, but if a woman chose to remain a deaconess and single, she could count on care in times of illness and in old age. These dedicated pioneers earned no salaries but, rather, worked in exchange for their living expenses and small stipends supplied by their institutional boards. The first trained deaconesses came from Chicago to Montana in 1898 to staff a small twenty-bed hospital in Great Falls. Chicago-trained Augusta Ariss arrived in 1902 to found the nursing school there. Deaconesses from the Chicago School also arrived to take charge of the Montana Deaconess School in Helena. From 1910 to the 1940s, it was the only Protestant-based boarding school west of the Mississippi. (It survives today as Intermountain, a treatment center for emotionally traumatized children.) Until the 1930s, deaconesses staffed the Great Falls hospital, its nursing school, and other deaconess hospitals in Glasgow, Sidney, Bozeman, Billings, Havre, and Butte. The Great Falls Deaconess Hospital evolved into today's Benefis Healthcare. The old Deaconess Hospital campus today serves a worthy purpose as an assisted living and memory care facility.

Sisters of Providence

Peter Ronan, for whom the town of Ronan was named, served as superintendent on the Flathead Reservation from 1877 to 1893. He and his wife, Mary, had close ties to St. Ignatius Mission.* Before the agency at Jocko had its own church built in 1889, the Ronans took their seven children on special feast days to worship at the mission. It was several days' journey, some seventeen miles away. Mary looked forward to these visits. Her husband and the little boys would stay in the house of the Jesuits while the Sisters of Providence welcomed Mary and her daughters. She came to count these grand women as good friends. The mother superior especially took Mary, whose own mother died when she was very small, under her wing. As a young wife and mother herself, it seemed to Mary that the efficient and selfless mother superior embodied all that a mother should be. "Those bright and precious visits," Mary wrote, "shine in my memory, comparable to the experience of the young matron who takes her children and goes into the peace and order and freedom from responsibilities that her own devoted mother's home affords. Always I was transported back to the dear days of my girlhood, to such a sense of quiet well being."

St. Helena Cathedral*

ON Christmas morning in 1914 promptly at ten o'clock, the fifteen bells in the St. Helena Cathedral spire rang out for the very first time, inviting all to the dedication mass. Fifteen hundred people filled the heavy oak pews to capacity. The service culminated a six-year building project. Patterned after the famous Votive Cathedral of the Sacred Heart in Vienna, Austria, the cathedral was designed by Austrian-born Albert O. Von Herbulis, who also designed St. Charles Hall at Carroll College. Still, the cathedral was unfinished and would not be entirely completed until 1924, but the community did not seem to notice the lack of stained glass windows and statuary so familiar today. The twenty-five-thousand-dollar pipe organ, installed days before, was a spectacular backdrop. The Right Reverend Bishop John B. Carroll conducted a memorable service, simple and poignant. The bishop noted the absence of those who had contributed so much. Peter Larson, whose passing the community mourned in 1908, was one major donor, and Thomas Cruse, who had died just a few days before, was the other. Cruse, wealthy founder of the Drumlummon Mine at Marysville, gave a third of the $650,000 building costs. He also paid for the fifteen bells—dedicated to his recently deceased daughter, Mamie. Cruse had followed every building phase, and his pride in the achievement matched that of Bishop Carroll himself. The day after the dedication, the first funeral Requiem Mass in the new cathedral was sung for Thomas Cruse.

House of the Good Shepherd*

On a cold day in February 1889, a small colony of Catholic Sisters of the Good Shepherd arrived in Helena from St. Paul, Minnesota. The white-robed sisters came to establish a safe haven for "wayward girls and fallen women" who wished to reform. The sisters settled in the house at the corner of Hoback and Ninth Street. In 1890, the small St. Helena's Catholic Church was built across Hoback, and the sisters added a dormitory next to the convent. During the 1890s, a priest said mass in German for the neighborhood immigrants at the tiny St. Helena Church. By 1900, nine sisters cared for twenty-seven residents between the ages of eight and thirty-six. In the dormitory basement, a state-of-the-art commercial laundry, added in 1904, provided job training and income. Neighbors were sometimes suspicious about what happened behind the high board fence. When one local father sent his fifteen-year-old daughter to the sisters because he could not control her behavior, the neighborhood rallied against him, burned an effigy of the man on his lawn, and chalked the vigilante warning 3-7-77 on his sidewalk. After all this uproar, the sisters returned the girl to her father. Tragically, she died of an undetected brain tumor a few months later. Doctors determined the tumor was the cause of her behavior problems. The home soon became overcrowded, and the complex moved to a larger facility on the west side. Church officials demolished the school in 1969, but the former gymnasium, all that remained, is today St. Andrew's Catholic School. On Hoback Street, the former dormitory now houses the studio of a prominent artist. The St. Helena Church across the street retains its original purpose, but the convent now houses apartments, and the sisters' adjoining Gothic Revival–style chapel is a neighborhood curiosity.

Ursuline Academy*

SIX teaching sisters of the Order of St. Ursula from Toledo, Ohio, came to Montana in 1884 at the invitation of the chaplain at Fort Keogh.* Their mission was to teach youth and establish schools for Indian children. Three of the sisters opened the first Ursuline convent in the Rocky Mountains in Miles City. The other "Lady Black Robes" established St. Labre's Mission among the Northern Cheyennes. In 1890, Ursuline sisters joined the Sisters of Providence at St. Ignatius.* When the homestead movement created a need for more urban educational facilities, the Great Falls Townsite Company offered the sisters any two city blocks. They chose a site overlooking the city for its tranquility, removed from the bustle of the city's center. In 1912, the Ursuline Academy opened its doors to day and boarding students of all denominations. The grand and noble building represents the culmination of the Ursulines' mission to bring education and culture to Montana's youth. The "Lady Black Robes" continued their mission teaching at the Academy until it became the Ursuline Centre in 1971. The Sisters who now reside within its lofty halls continue to serve in the community and graciously open their home to ecumenical activities.

Canton Church*

SETTLEMENTS like the small village of Canton sprang up in the 1860s to serve ranchers and farmers in the Missouri River Valley. By 1872, Canton boasted a mercantile, post office, saloon and dance hall, doctor, and hotel. Scattered settlers came together to build a simple, eloquent church. Paid for with community donations and built by ninety volunteer lay laborers, the church was dedicated in 1876. St. Joseph's Church is Montana's oldest standing Roman Catholic church not built by a religious order. Its arched windows, fanlight over the entry, and ornamental moldings are rare and reflect the roots of many local settlers who hailed from Canton, New York, and elsewhere back East. The Northern Pacific bypassed Canton in the 1880s, but the congregation continued to grow. After World War II, federal officials planned to upgrade Canyon Ferry Dam and raise the reservoir. Canton lay in its path. In 1952, St. Joseph's Church was moved two and a half miles to its present location on Route 284 near Townsend before water swallowed the land. The church became a focal point for the displaced community. The Canton Church Project, organized in 1996, maintains the church. Its members include descendants of the original pioneer congregation.

Marysville Church*

MARYSVILLE'S Methodist Episcopal Church is a familiar local landmark. Built in 1886 by its congregation on land purchased from Marysville's founder Thomas Cruse, the modest clapboard-sided church and its bell tower reflect a period of heady growth. The Northern Pacific Railroad had reached Marysville earlier in the year, bringing with it a steady supply of machine-milled building materials. Crude cabins of rough-hewn lumber quickly gave way to more modern buildings. By the 1890s, the population reached five thousand, and Cruse's mine, sold to English capitalists in 1882, was on its way to producing an astounding 20 million dollars in silver and gold. But production dwindled, and by 1939, the modest little church was abandoned and near the point of collapse. In 1967, Margaret and John Hollow, whose grandparents John E. O'Brien and Ellen O'Grady were married there in 1887, bought the derelict old building. In the years since, the family has lovingly restored the church, its windows and frames, and many of its furnishings to their original simple grace. Today, the church's stark silhouette is a favorite of painters and photographers.

Temple Emanu El*

✴ OPPORTUNITY drew European Jewish immigrants to the gold camp at Last Chance, where business and religion brought them together. The Jewish community contributed a firm financial foundation to the early settlement. It was the Jewish pioneers, especially, with ties to resources in larger cities, whose businesses rose again and again in the face of ruinous fires that plagued early Helena. Helena's Jews worshipped together as early as 1866, yet the congregation remained without a temple for over twenty years. In 1890, the public gathered as Governor Joseph K. Toole ceremoniously laid the cornerstone for the first Jewish temple between St. Paul and Portland. Helena architects Heinlen and Matthias drew the plans for the Romanesque and Moorish style of synagogue under the tutelage of a building committee. Strong Eastern influences include keyhole windows and star-studded domes that once capped the corner towers. The grand temple reflected the congregation's generous intent "to ornament the city" that had become home. But the congregation dwindled by the 1930s and the State of Montana acquired the building, promising to use it for social purposes. Religious symbolism removed and a second story added, the former temple became an early model of adaptive reuse. It housed Social and Rehabilitative Services until 1976 and then lay vacant until the Catholic Diocese of Helena purchased the building in 1981. On April 21, 2002, descendants of Jewish pioneers and the Catholic community together celebrated the centennial of this regional landmark. The Hebrew date on the cornerstone, 5651, documents its original purpose.

In War and Peace

*Fort Shaw**

✳ ROBERT GOULD SHAW, the son of wealthy Boston abolition-ists, led the famous Massachusetts Fifty-fourth Regiment during the Civil War. This was the first African American regiment, formed after Abraham Lincoln's Emancipation Proclamation in 1863 allowed blacks to serve in the military as volunteers. African Americans came to offer their services from all over the North and the Caribbean. They proved their mettle under Colonel Shaw during the famous attack on Fort Wagner in South Carolina. On July 18, 1863, more than seventy enlisted men and three officers fell in battle. Colonel Shaw also lost his life. The movie *Glory,* starring Matthew Broderick, tells the story, which is a significant part of Civil War history. A few years after the Fort Wagner attack, the U.S. government in 1867 founded Fort Shaw on the Montana frontier at Sun River. First named Fort Reynolds, it was renamed to honor Colonel Shaw. Fort Shaw protected miners and settlers traveling through the area during a time of Blackfeet raids and heightened hostili-ties. General John Gibbon rode out from Fort Shaw in 1876 to join General George Custer and the Seventh Cavalry at the Battle of the Little Bighorn. Decommissioned in 1891, the fort then served as a boarding school for Indian children. The famous Fort Shaw girls' basketball team captured national attention between 1902 and 1906 with their winning streak, taking the title of "World Champions." The campus includes one large and impressive adobe-and-frame building from the 1860s.

Fort C. F. Smith*

JOHN JACOBS and John Bozeman carved a route from the Oregon Trail to the Montana gold camps in 1863, cutting through native hunting grounds. It was a very dangerous route. Ruts of the Bozeman Trail still mark the vicinity of Fort C. F. Smith in the Bighorn Canyon National Recreation Area in Bighorn County. This early fort and post cemetery, along with Forts Phil Kearny and Reno in Wyoming, functioned as military posts to guard the wagon route and the early miners and settlers coming into Montana Territory. Named for Major General Charles Ferguson Smith, it was one of the first military posts in Montana. Colonel Henry B. Carrington constructed Fort C. F. Smith in the summer of 1866. Nearby, in summer 1867, Red Cloud with one thousand Sioux attacked a haying party of soldiers. In what was later known as the Hayfield Fight, twenty-five soldiers defended themselves with newly arrived Springfield breech-loading rifles. The short-lived fort closed in 1868. Traces of the limestone quarry used to construct the fort, along with remnant foundations, remain. In 1892, the soldiers buried there were moved to the Custer National Cemetery.

Rosebud Battlefield*

ROSEBUD BATTLEFIELD STATE PARK, twenty-five miles east of Crow Agency near the Wyoming border, is Montana's newest National Historic Landmark. The state park is the site of one of the nation's largest Indian battles. There were twenty-five hundred participants in this prelude to the stunning defeat of General George A. Custer at Little Bighorn eight days later. Sioux and Northern

Cheyenne Indians who had fled the reservation gathered in this area in spring 1876. By June, there were lodges housing as many as fifteen thousand people, among them some three thousand to four thousand warriors. On June 17, 1876, some 750 Sioux and Cheyennes under Crazy Horse attacked General George Crook, setting the stage for the Indians' victory over Custer at Little Bighorn. The Indians withdrew after the six-hour battle with a loss of only thirteen warriors to the army's approximately seventy casualties. The Rosebud battle effectively took General Crook's troops out of the campaign. Rosebud Battlefield State Park is rich in archaeological features, including a buffalo jump used by native people for thousands of years, tipi rings, rock cairns, and high-density habitation sites. The park is also a place where scholars come to study military strategies. At the end of the grass-choked path at the top of the hill, the visitor cannot help but draw in a breath, taking in sweeping panoramic views of the prairie and snow-capped Bighorn Mountains.

Bear Paw Battlefield*

SIXTEEN miles south of Chinook along the windswept Montana High Line, hikers can follow a self-guided trail through an undeveloped landscape. It was in that area on September 30, 1877, that General Nelson Miles attacked Chief Joseph's camp. Joseph and more than four hundred weary men, women, and children had stopped there to rest. Fleeing their Idaho homeland with soldiers in pursuit, the Nez Perce were just forty miles from their destination at the Canadian border. They might have been successful, but the soldiers stole most of their horses. Nez Perce marksmen did, however, inflict some sixty casualties upon the soldiers, many of them officers. After a six-day siege, Chief Joseph surrendered. The Bear Paw surrender brought an end to Joseph's Nez Perces as an independent Indian people. They lived miserably as displaced persons in Kansas and Oklahoma Territory, where hundreds died of malnutrition and starvation. Later, they shared the Colville Reservation in Washington. Although Chief Joseph's famous statement, "I will fight no more forever," is likely fiction, his surrender is one of history's most tragic events. The battlefield is a National Historic Landmark and part of the Nez Perce National Historic Trail, which starts in Joseph, Oregon, and follows the path of the Nez Perce flight. The battlefield marks the end of the trail.

Fort Keogh*

FORT KEOGH was established in July 1876 in the few weeks following the Custer loss at Little Bighorn. The army cavalry post takes its name from Captain Myles Keogh, who served under Custer and died in the battle. The fort's commander was General Nelson Miles. In 1879, Miles City—whose name honors the general—became the first seat of Custer County, and the fort grew to be one of the largest in the territory. Sixty buildings once sprawled across the diamond-shaped grounds. In 1907, the army withdrew its infantry troops, and in 1909, the fort became a remount station where the army trained and shipped horses worldwide. The army shipped more horses from Fort Keogh during World War I than from any other army post. The military withdrew in 1924 and transferred the land to the U.S. Department of Agriculture for experimental stock raising and the growing of forage crops. This work continues today. The remains of the historic fort include the parade ground, 1883 wagon shed, 1887 flagpole, and seven other pre-1924 structures.

Fort Missoula*

FORT MISSOULA, established in 1877, brought a non-combative military presence to western Montana. The fort's service was long and diverse. From 1888 to 1898, the black

Twenty-fifth Infantry Regiment was stationed at the fort. Twenty of the men explored potential military applications of the bicycle, riding nineteen hundred miles to St. Louis in forty days. During the Spanish-American conflict in 1898, the fort garrisoned volunteers known as Grigsby's Cowboys. Eighteen buildings added between 1904 and 1912 form the core of the present complex. During World War I, the fort provided technical training. Between 1933 and 1941, Fort Missoula was the nation's largest Civilian Conservation Corps regional headquarters, employing two hundred thousand men. During World War II, it was the nation's largest civilian detention camp interning Japanese Americans and Italian nationals. Japanese internees were mostly Japanese-American businessmen unjustly under suspicion because of their Japanese ancestry. Most Italian internees were staff on cruise ships anchored off-shore in U.S. water. They affectionately dubbed the fort "Bella Vista." After World War II, the fort served as a medium-security army prison. The buildings were closed in 1948, but adaptability and community involvement have assured them an active future.

Rinzo Ogata

RINZO OGATA was a longtime rancher in the Helena Valley and the Japanese vice counsel for the Helena area. Ogata and his wife raised seven children, one of whom received a Purple Heart for service in the Pacific during World War II. The Ogata children placed this message on the family monument in Forestvale Cemetery*: "To Mother and Father from our President. See his belated words of empathy, 1999." A brass plaque at the back of the monument reproduces a letter from President Bill Clinton following the passage of the Civil Liberties Act of 1998. It reads in part: "More than 50 years ago the U.S. government unjustly interned, evacuated, or otherwise deprived of liberty, you and many other Japanese Americans. On behalf of all Americans, I offer a sincere apology for the actions that unfairly denied Japanese Americans and their families fundamental liberties during WORLD WAR II." President Clinton concludes, ". . . we must learn from the past and dedicate ourselves to renewing strength, justice, and freedom. Together we can guarantee a better future for generations to come."

Fort Assinniboine*

✳ BUILDINGS with hollow windows sparsely dot the great expanse of flat grassland. A few still-used buildings lie hidden from view, allowing a glimpse of another time. Fort Assinniboine was once the largest military fort in Montana, strategically placed along the route called the Old Forts Trail, which linked Montana's Fort Benton with Forts Walsh and Battleford in Saskatchewan, Canada. Founded in 1879, its eight hundred soldiers commanded such a presence that only a low board fence enclosed it. Natural adversity, including disease, accidents, bad water, extreme weather, fire ants, and swarms of mosquitoes, proved worse than human threats. Although under warning many times, Fort Assinniboine saw no direct action. Famed general Black Jack Pershing came to the remote post in 1895 as a first lieutenant in the Tenth Cavalry, a unit of African American soldiers. Pershing's nickname derives from this period in his career. Pershing met General Nelson Miles at Fort Assinniboine, and because of their friendship, Pershing won a position as instructor at West Point. Fort Assinniboine's unmarried officers' quarters where Pershing once lived still stands, a grand red brick structure with a turreted tower. In 1911, the last soldiers departed, abandoning the fort to the elements. In 1915, the State of Montana purchased the buildings still standing along with some two thousand acres. The federal government auctioned off the rest of the military reserve. In 1916, the state turned the property over to the Northern Montana College of Havre for use as an agricultural experiment station. Part of the historic fort remains in use.

Fort Harrison

⁂ THE meeting of the Great Northern and Northern Pacific lines was strategic in placing Fort Benjamin Harrison west of Helena in 1892. Named after the twenty-third president of the United States (1889–1893), the post was renamed Fort William Henry Harrison in honor of Benjamin's grandfather, the ninth president of the United States. Benjamin Harrison's son, Russell, had served a term as head of Helena's federal assay office in the 1880s. The fort remained an active army post until 1913. With the U.S. involvement in World War I, the Montana Regiment of the National Guard assembled at Fort Harrison in 1917, and, in 1919, the U.S. Public Health Service took over management of the fort. At the start of World War II, President Franklin D. Roosevelt activated the First Special Service Force (FSSF), an elite group of Canadian and American army personnel. After training at Fort Harrison, the FSSF served with distinction in both the Pacific and European theaters. General Douglas MacArthur had "the greatest affection and admiration" for Montana's 163rd. Fort Harrison today is the site of the Veterans Affairs Medical and Regional Office Center providing medical care to veterans of all branches of the service.

Montana's National Guard

⁂ THE Dick Act created the National Guard in 1903, reorganizing state militias into National Guard units. However, Montana's territorial legislature authorized a National Guard in 1885. Since then, Montana guardsmen have aided in a variety of causes. They assisted with the 1894 Butte riots, the devastating wildfires of 1910, and the 1914 Butte miners' strike. They were mustered into service for the Spanish-American War in 1898, suffered casualties during the 1899 Philippine Insurrection, and guarded the U.S.–Mexican border against Pancho Villa's incursions in 1916.

Montana guardsmen fought in France during World War I and participated in island operations in the Pacific Theater throughout the war. Following this long tradition of service, 1,100 Montana soldiers and airmen have been deployed annually since September 11, 2001, to serve in operations Noble Eagle, Enduring Freedom, and Iraqi Freedom. The historic National Guard Armory* at Lyndale and North Last Chance Gulch in Helena, built in 1942, now houses state offices, but it is a bold reminder of the Montana Guard's contributions and sacrifices both at home and abroad.

Red Cross Quilts

As Americans agonized over their soldiers on the front in 1917, a quilting revival took wing. Women's magazines encouraged quilters with the slogan: "Make quilts—save the blankets for our boys over there." Individuals and organizations expressed their patriotism by stitching quilts for the Red Cross. Thousands of these comfort quilts went to Europe to the victims of World War I. Stitching comfort quilts at home was a way to support the war effort, and Montanans were especially involved. Also at this dark time, communities and organizations created hundreds of signature Red Cross quilts as fund-raisers. The Ladies Auxiliary of the United Commercial Travelers in Great Falls made one of these quilts in 1918. According to practice, businesses or individuals purchased space to have their names embroidered on the quilt. Prices for a space ranged from twenty-five cents to one hundred dollars depending on where the name was placed. Auxiliary members donated the materials, did all the sewing and quilting, and stitched more than thirteen hundred names on the front and back. They then raffled the quilt, hoping to make one thousand dollars. They did even better, and in December of 1918, a total of $1,060.80 went to the Cascade County Chapter of the American Red Cross. These quilts often came back to their makers. In 1926, the Ladies Auxiliary purchased the quilt from the raffle winner and, a few years later, gifted it to the Montana Historical Society, where it is part of the museum collection.

Horace W. Bivins

HORACE W. BIVINS was born in Virginia of free ancestry and was college educated. He enlisted in the Tenth Cavalry, the famous Buffalo Soldiers, in 1887 as a noncommissioned officer. Bivins served in Arizona in campaigns against Geronimo. The Tenth Cavalry was reassigned to Fort Custer in Montana. There Bivins became famous as such an expert marksman that Buffalo Bill Cody tried to entice him to travel with his show. Bivins preferred the military. He was a veteran of two Cuban wars and three Philippine engagements. At the attack on San Juan Hill, he fought beside Teddy Roosevelt's Rough Riders and later received the Silver Star for his heroic actions. Some years later when Roosevelt visited Billings, he was disappointed to learn that Bivins was not at home but at Camp Dix, New Jersey, commanding a labor battalion. Bivins retired in 1913 and reenlisted at personal hardship in 1918 during World War I, retiring a second time as captain in 1919. Bivins's record for marksmanship stood until the 1970s, and today remains one of the all-time highest. During his thirty-two-year career in the military, Bivins received thirty-two medals, one for every year of service. Bivins studied taxidermy at the University of Minnesota, practiced that for a while, and did extensive truck gardening in the Billings area, where he lived a long, quiet life.

War Games

BRANCHES of the military heightened their collegiate recruiting efforts in the aftermath of World War I. Mount St. Charles College in Helena, today's Carroll College, was a boys' school back then and one of many institutions that supported the effort to build up troops depleted during the recent war. On a winter day in 1920, recruiting officers staged the liveliest mock battle Montana has ever seen. The *Butte Miner* reported that the officers brought in the burly Ermentraude, the biggest, toughest, rudest lady in Montana and a match for any regiment. She broke laws and violated the peace. Perhaps fed some kind of illicit gasoline, Ermentraude ran amok, chasing battalions of young college cadets out of their dugouts, pushing over a number of trees, and thrusting her snubby nose under the porch of an old frame residence, which she overturned without hesitation. While the young cadets awoke the town with their practice volleys and battle cries, hundreds of young boys climbed the hillsides to cheer them on. The noise echoed throughout the Helena Valley as the young cadets, although soundly beaten, remained defiant. The *Miner* observed that neither all of Governor Stewart's horses nor all his men could put the demolished house back together again. The exercise was a success. The Lady Ermentraude, of course, was a veteran army tank.

Lewistown Airfield*

AFTER the attack on Pearl Harbor in 1941, the U.S. Army selected Great Falls as the site of a major air base with satellite airfields at Cut Bank, Glasgow, and Lewistown. In October 1942, the first Boeing B-17 Flying Fortresses roared over Lewistown's Main Street with their bomb bays open, buzzed the treetops, and landed at the Lewistown Airfield. Crews trained day and night, familiarizing themselves with all aspects of the B-17. They also trained with the top-secret Norden bombsight, a computerized aiming device that reportedly could "put bombs in a pickle barrel." After training, aircrews flew directly to join the air war in Europe. Nearly one thousand GIs trained at Lewistown. The men endeared themselves to the community, and many married local girls. A number of the servicemen never came home. B-17s carried four thousand pounds of bombs, serving in every World War II combat zone, and casualties were horrific. One mission over Germany claimed sixty B-17s and six hundred lives. Recently listed in the National Register, the Lewistown Airfield's survival is a rarity, and its intact Norden bombsight storage shelter is the only known identifiable example remaining in the United States.

Glasgow Airfield*

DURING World War II, Army airmen trained on the Boeing B-17 Flying Fortress at the satellite airfield in Glasgow, one of four Montana bases built for this purpose. Other airfields were at Great Falls, Lewistown, and Cut Bank. In 1942, on the first anniversary of Pearl Harbor, B-17 heavy bombers arrived in Glasgow to complete the final phase of essential aerial combat training. Army reporter Vernon Hamilton of the *Red Devil News* wrote:

> From Glasgow's airport on the hill
> Bombers take off and land at will
> Day or night it's all the same
> Pilots learning war's grim game

During the year 1943, the men learned formation flying, navigation, gunnery, and bombing. The "Red Devils" of the 96th, "Van's Valiants" of the 549th, "Wittan's Wallopers" of the 568th, and the "Lucky Devils" of the 614th bomb squadrons each trained in turn at Glasgow. These squadrons served in Europe and North Africa and received presidential citations for their gallant and heroic missions.

St. Marie

FOURTEEN miles north of U.S. Highway 2 on Montana Highway 24 is the abandoned Glasgow Air Force Base. U.S.

airmen trained at the base from 1955 until it closed in 1968. A few miles farther up the highway is the town of St. Marie. The little community was built to house the airmen and their families. A drive through this modern ghost town where seventy-two hundred people once lived is like a trip back in time to the 1960s. There are blocks of empty streets and abandoned buildings where families once barbecued in the yards and visited with neighbors. Swings sit idle on the playground where children laughed and played. Although the buildings may be dilapidated, there has been no vandalism, and only a few broken windows let in the rain and snow. Solidly constructed, the housing units have garages, basements, and hardwood floors. Despite the quiet streets and empty yards, nearly two hundred people do live in St. Marie, which is a far cry from its peak population. If you are looking for bargain real estate, you can buy a vintage 1960 housing unit for around fifteen to twenty thousand dollars. It's like buying a condo—you fix up the inside, and the St. Marie Village Association maintains the outside. The only drawback is that it's a little bit like living in the Twilight Zone.

Spirited History

Elinor Knott

✳ ELINOR KNOTT was one of the many madams at the Dumas Hotel* in Butte. On a winter night in 1955, Knott packed her suitcase, put on her hat, and sat down to wait. Her lover had promised to leave his wife and come for her. They would leave Butte to start a new life together. But the next morning a friend discovered Knott's body in her rooms at the Dumas. The coroner pronounced her dead of natural causes. Dark whispers among acquaintances suggested that something was amiss. Although officials declared her destitute, friends knew Knott owned jewelry, a red Cadillac, and a Harley Davidson motorcycle. These never surfaced, and there was no inquest into her death. The coroner pronounced it suicide by a lethal combination of alcohol and drugs. A few years ago, a woman who had worked at the Dumas in the 1970s returned to Butte on a visit. She told of a curious experience. She said she was staying alone at the Dumas one night. She was in the bathroom upstairs at the end of the hall, with the door open. She had a clear view of the hall and the corner stairway. She saw a woman wearing a hat and carrying a suitcase walk past the bathroom door and descend the stairs. She was so shocked she didn't move until the top of the woman's head disappeared. She hurried down the stairs after her, but there was no sign of the woman. The front and back doors were

146

locked and barred shut. Some time later, an artist commissioned to paint a mural for the city of Butte rented Knott's former apartment to use as a studio. Something compelled her to paint portrait after portrait of a woman she had never seen. She couldn't seem to paint anything else. One of the canvasses, rescued from the trash, shows a middle-aged woman with a coy smile and a quaint little hat.

Flathead Lake

SETTLEMENT of the remote Flathead Lake region lagged behind the rest of Montana Territory because travel there was so difficult. The advent of the Northern Pacific across Montana in 1883 made access more feasible. Beginning in 1885, steamboats plied the waters of Flathead Lake, carrying goods and passengers between Polson and Demersville, the early settlement that later relocated to become present-day Kalispell. Settlers and visitors traveled to the Flathead Lake country via the Northern Pacific to Ravalli. From Ravalli Station, named for Father Anthony Ravalli of nearby St. Mary's Mission,* stagecoaches ran to Polson three times a week. One of the lake's first steamers, the *U. S. Grant*, was a little converted sailboat outfitted with a donkey engine and a screw-type propeller. Its captain was James C. Kerr, a veteran pilot of the Great Lakes. Captain Kerr skippered Flathead steamers from 1886 until his death at the helm of the *Klondyke* in 1909. In 1889 aboard the *U. S. Grant*, Captain Kerr and his passengers saw a twenty-foot object swimming directly in the steamer's path. This was the first recorded sighting of the mysterious creature that some believe lurks in the deep waters of Flathead Lake.

Flathead Monster

MANY believe that a monster lurks in the deep waters of Flathead Lake. Even Whitefish native and noted author Dorothy

Johnson believed that there is something out there. Ken Soderberg of Montana State Parks relates an incident that Maintenance Supervisor Merle Phillips shared with him a few years ago. Phillips and his crew went to Wild Horse Island to dispose of a dead horse. Sometimes dynamite can be used to obliterate a large carcass, but a nearby cabin made that solution unwise. They improvised a raft of inflated inner tubes and boards. They lashed the horse to the boards, legs sticking straight up, but miscalculated its weight. The raft partially submerged in the water with only the horse's legs sticking out. As the crew slowly towed the horse, passing boaters did double takes. Finally one boater turned around, pulled alongside, and asked, "Hey, what are you guys doing?" Phillips replied, "Stay back from this official boat." But the driver persisted, "Yeah, but what are you doing?" The look on the fellow's face was priceless when Phillips replied, "We're trolling for the Flathead Lake monster!" While this incident may be amusing, from the earliest times the Kootenai Indians had a special name for Flathead Lake and must have known something we do not. They called it "Monster Lake."

Ghost Train

THE train came gliding up the tracks between Hamilton and Grantsdale in January 1893. At the same place each night it chugged along, smoke pouring from the engine. But there was no clacking of the rails as steel met steel and no melancholy whistle echoing through the valley. Silent as the mist, the ghost train slid on its route through the Bitterroot Valley, night after night. Farmer Louis Pennoyer was the only witness to the phantom train. No one called him crazy when he reported it. His fellow farmers respected the young family man who had no reason to fabricate such a strange tale. Pennoyer said that the scene was always the same. Just after dusk, when evening cast its shadows over the winter fields lying fallow, over the farmhouses dotting the valley, and over horses and cows in their pastures, the train sped past. The lantern winked in the dark, illuminating a crewman who frantically swung his lantern as if warning of some dire event. Then the man disappeared inside as if the car had swallowed him without a trace. The train continued its silent glide along the tracks until it was lost in the darkness. The valley buzzed with speculation, wondering what it meant. But the misty vision never came clear, and Pennoyer's vision faded into obscurity.

Haunted Homestead

An abandoned homestead near Chester in Liberty County lies tucked in a grassy hollow beside a swift creek where huge old cottonwood trees stand sentinel. The emerald oasis served generations of Native Americans traveling across the prairie into seasonal hunting grounds. Along this travel corridor, such irrigated sanctuaries were few and far between. It was therefore sacred ground. Homesteaders built upon this sanctuary. Such a beautiful, well-watered place, they thought, would bring them prosperity. They were wrong. The original homesteader was reputed to be a tyrant who hired sheepherders and killed them rather than pay their wages. The once-lovely house has long stood empty, its walls defaced, and all that made it homey gone. Some twenty-five years ago, local teens planned to spend a night in the house. They spread out their bedrolls, shut the one remaining door against the nighttime chill, and settled down to talk. The door flew open with a crash. There was no wind. The boys again shut the door, this time placing a large rock securely against it. They settled down again. Whap! The rock whizzed past their heads and hit the wall. The boys fled. To this day the shell of the house stands, a poignant ruin. But it's not a place to linger.

Deer Lodge Prison*

✦ THE historic prison at Deer Lodge served Montana from 1870 during territorial days until 1979. Today it is a museum, but over the course of more than a century, thousands of prisoners lost their identities within its walls. Some horrific events occurred there. One took place on March 8, 1908, when George Rock and W. A. Hayes attacked Warden Frank Conley and his chief deputy, James Robinson, in an attempted escape. Conley shot both Rock and Hayes, hitting Rock in the head and Hayes twice, once through each lung. These shots should have been fatal, but the bullets stopped neither man. The two prisoners were still able to fatally slit Robinson's throat with a pocketknife and slash Conley so severely it took 103 stitches to close the wounds. Conley carefully nursed Rock and Hayes so that they would be healthy when, convicted of murder, both were hanged in the prison yard as an example to the other men. These were the only hangings within the walls, but not the only violent deaths. And the prison is a place that captured men's souls. Little wonder that both visitors and staff report the sounds of murmuring voices, the doors of empty cells clanging shut, the sounds of heavy boots patrolling the cell blocks, and unseen hands plucking at their clothing.

Virginia City Ghosts

✦ VIRGINIA CITY is one of Montana's most haunted places. Nearly every building has a story attached. Helena resident Vicki Smith, a vivacious, charming veteran of the Virginia City Players, tells of an odd encounter she had in the Virginia City opera house. Smith had gone to the theater to critique a variety show rehearsal at the request of a friend. The rehearsal was under way, and Smith quietly entered the theater. She had her pick of seats as there were no other observers seated in the house. She took one of the roomy padded leather aisle seats. As she sat there quietly, Smith suddenly heard a *"whoosh"* in the seat next to her, like someone sat down on a whoopee cushion. The seats in the opera house, once plush, are now worn and squashy. Smith looked over and saw a depression in the cushion, as if someone were sitting there. She could see no one there, yet she felt a person there, and as she sat next to him or her, she wondered what she should do. She sat very still. Then suddenly whoever, or whatever, it was got up, and she watched the seat return to normal. Smith's good friend, the late Barbara Brook, also had an experience in the opera house. She once entered the empty theater and heard someone singing in a most beautiful voice. The song was in a foreign language, and it drew her to it like the Pied Piper. Though Barbara searched the premises, the phantom singer could not be found. Over the years, others have reported that they too have heard the beguiling, ghostly singer.

Grant-Kohrs* Cowboys

MATT CONNOR worked as a ranger at the Grant-Kohrs Ranch. On Halloween 2001, Connor was locking up the buildings for the evening. He made his usual security checks. As he passed the 1870s draft horse barn, he saw that the door was padlocked. But when he made his final check, he saw the door standing wide open. Connor stepped into the barn, saw nothing amiss, and pulled the door shut. As he fiddled with the padlock, he heard the sound of cowboy boots on the barn floor, on the other side of the door. He distinctly heard two sets of cowboy boots and two men in the barn, talking in low tones. As Connor stood with his ear to the entry, he heard the top of the grain bin, just on the other side of the door, flip open and bang in his ear. He heard the scoop hit the grain. Then he heard the cowboy dip deeply into it, get a hefty scoopful, and dump it into a waiting bucket. Connor undid the padlock, pushed open the door, and again entered the barn. No one was there, and the grain bin was empty. As Connor again shut and began to lock the door, he heard the mumbling cowboys and realized that this was no ordinary event. He left the door open. He never again heard them in the barn, but during his time at the Grant-Kohrs Ranch, he always kept the barn open on Halloween.

Copper King Mansion*

✦ A group of friends sat around the dining room table one evening at the Copper King Mansion, once the home of William A. Clark. Suddenly they heard a strange moaning sound. It started out low, gathered strength, then ended abruptly. Again came the low-pitched moan from some deep place within the house. They knew it was coming from the third floor and that someone would have to investigate. The thought filled them with dread. They agreed to go together. As they ascended the grand staircase, one step at a time, the sound rose and fell like a ghastly, ghoulish greeting. They reached the third floor, and the moaning had risen to a deafening, all-encompassing crescendo. It was loud, it was eerie, and it left the eight adults clutching one another. The monstrous, groaning sigh ebbed and died, but rose again immediately. They flung open the door to the ballroom and stopped at once and stared. A pipe organ stood against one wall. Outside, the wind was blowing, and it whistled into the ballroom through a small broken pane of stained glass. The realization began to dawn. The wind's target was a bass pipe, and the death-rattle moan was only the rise and fall of the wind hitting a low note!

Dorothy Dunn

✦ SPIRITS shroud the ghost town of Bannack, where sluices once ran and whiskey flowed. Vigilantes bestowed violent beginnings. But dig deeper. The town's windswept cemetery where spirits rest, or don't rest, is evidence of tragedies even more indelible than hangings and shootings. In August 1916, sixteen-year-old Dorothy Dunn, her cousin Fern, and a friend waded into a dredge pond and stepped off a shelf into deep water. None could swim. A passerby saved Fern and her friend, but lovely, vivacious Dorothy drowned. The site of the accident to this day is known as Dorothy's Hole. Bertie Mathews, whose parents ran the Meade Hotel,* took the death of her best friend Dorothy very hard. Some time after the tragedy, Bertie was upstairs in the hotel when she saw the apparition of her friend. Bertie recognized Dorothy's long blue dress. The experience scared her, and she seldom talked about it. Since then, many others have seen Dorothy upstairs in the hotel. Visitors report cold spots, and children who know nothing of Dorothy claim to have talked with a girl in a long blue dress.

Mine Spooks

WAINO NYLAND came to Butte as a child from Finland in the early 1900s. He remembered that the first disaster his family experienced occurred when a lever broke on a hoisting engine as a cage was taking four men down into the mines. The cage fell twenty-two hundred feet, killing the riders. The bodies of the four men, one of them Nyland's next-door neighbor, came out of the wreckage in pieces. The men's spirits, according to Nyland, still haunt the mine. If you look down the shaft when the time is right on certain days, four pairs of lonely eyes stare back at you, looking up from the bottom of their deep, dark grave. Most don't like to talk about ghosts, but all Butte miners have heard unexplained noises deep in the mines, had shovels or buckets disappear, and know about the phantom ring. Every hoisting engineer has answered a ring for a hoist-up where no one is working. If he sends a cage down in answer to the ring, it invariably comes back empty. And all miners know to watch out for the white goat on Anaconda Hill. He can turn up anywhere, because all Butte mines are connected, and sneak up from behind. If you are too close to the edge of a shaft, he'll butt you right in.

St. Albert's Hall

✴ ST. ALBERT'S HALL at Carroll College was built in 1924 for twelve Dominican sisters who came from Germany to take over campus food services. The selfless sisters were homesick, and they used to joke that they were so poor they couldn't buy a stamp to send a letter home. Although stories circulate throughout all the dorms about a motherly nun who visits sick students, St. Albert's Hall is where some have actually been introduced to the Dominican sisters. The former convent later became a student dormitory, and for a time it housed the campus radio station. Students who did radio broadcasts from St. Albert's were familiar with the nuns. The radio show would begin at 6:30 on Sunday mornings. Promptly at 6:30, footsteps would begin at the head of the hallway, setting a deliberate pace, the same every time. There was a pause at each door down the hall as the footsteps came closer. When they paused at the studio door, students say that they could always *feel* someone on the other side of the door looking in. Students generally believed that this was the Mother Superior's morning wakeup routine, enacted so many times over the decades without varying that it continued long after the nuns left the campus in 1961.

Centerville Ghost

✴ BUTTE's Dublin Gulch in Centerville was home to many Irish transplants. Tales of banshees and ghosts carried across the Atlantic influenced the community. In Butte, it didn't take much to fuel imaginations when the Grim Reaper could come at any moment. This is why the Centerville ghost caused such panic. It began late one night in 1901, when two young men approached a black-clad figure on the hill above Center Street. They first thought it might be a robber, but as they came closer, the figure threw back his black veil. Blue streaks of sulfur illuminated its horribly distorted features. It uttered a piercing scream, turned, and fled down the track. Sightings were numerous, and the "Dark Ghost of Centerville" became the topic over every back fence in Butte. Weeks later, the newspapers put the spirit to rest, hinting that the whole thing was a prank and predicting that someone would come forward to take credit. But no one did. Two decades later, those who had been youngsters back in 1901 now had children of their own, and they still shivered at memory of the Centerville ghost. In 1922, newsman "Silver Dick" Butler claimed that he made the story up. In 1930, laundryman Joe Duffy said he did it. Do these men deserve credit for creating the ghost? Or was there a seed of truth to the story? Perhaps the real explanation is a combination of the two.

Finger in the Door

A house in Helena's southeast neighborhood was long home to Annabelle Richards and her family. Annabelle loved the spirits that lived there, but others were not so tolerant. When the Richards family moved to Washington, D.C., for a period of years, a series of tenants lived in the house. Annabelle never learned exactly what the spirits did to frighten her tenants. Long after Annabelle moved out of the house, however, one of them related this incident. A mother and her five-year-old daughter briefly rented the house. The mother was afraid the lock on her daughter's bedroom door might malfunction, so she took the doorknob off the door, leaving a hole where it had been. The child always slept with her cat curled up by her side. One night she awoke, and the cat wasn't there. She searched the room and finally saw him at the foot of her bed with his eyes fixed on something. The cat's eyes got bigger and bigger, and her fright grew. She knew she would have to see what her cat was staring at so intently. So she gathered up all the courage she could and followed her cat's gaze. What she saw gave her nightmares for years to come. The cat's eyes rested upon the place where the doorknob used to be. Sticking through the hole was a finger, and *it was pointing directly at her.*

Quartz Street Fire Station*

BUTTE's Quartz Street Fire Station has a past that refuses to be forgotten. Built in 1900, the station housed twenty-two men, Chief Peter Sanger, and his family. Sanger's first wife, Margaret, died in the family's apartment in 1904. He remarried in 1908, and his second wife, Louisa, like Margaret before her, took up a post by the window where she watched for her husband's safe return. In January 1915, Sanger's truck collided with a Walkerville streetcar en route to an alarm. Hundreds attended his funeral at the station. After several more generations of firefighters had come and gone, the station became the Butte–Silver Bow Public Archives in 1981. Traces of its past include a wall of long-disconnected alarm boxes installed by Chief Sanger. Archivists and volunteers can tell you that they have heard the disconnected alarm bells clang as if the firemen never left. After the building has closed and darkness edges in, some say you can hear the men banter back and forth, reenacting scenes played out in the past hundreds of times. One late afternoon, the building was empty, and the director was out in the parking lot. She was certain she saw an older woman gazing out the east window, drying her hands on a dish towel. Some time later, a photograph of Louisa Sanger came to light. She was standing in the same window, drying her hands on a dish towel, gazing out to the street. Recent major renovations have erased the tangible elements of the former station. Time will tell if the work has erased the spirits, too.

Art, Entertainment, Travel,
and Leisure

Horse Racing

✳ NATIVE AMERICANS brought horses into Montana in the 1700s, and racing early on became a common sport. The tiny town of Racetrack near Deer Lodge takes its name from the long straightaway where, according to local tradition, Indians raced their ponies. Johnny Grant made the early miners' racing circuits. In November 1864, Grant advertised in the *Montana Post* that his mare, Limber Belle, would race anywhere in the territory. Billy Bay, a Kentucky thoroughbred stallion, was the first thoroughbred to appear by name in Montana's written record. Blackfeet brought the horse into the territory from north of the Great Salt Lake. Trader Malcolm Clarke then acquired Billy Bay through his Blackfeet in-laws. Money, furs, and other valuables had been staked on Billy Bay in intertribal races. Horse racing was a popular sport among the miners, and races in the streets of the camps were common pastimes on their days off. Virginia Slade acquired the far-famed Billy Bay from Malcolm Clarke and was a frequent contender in the weekly Sunday races held in the streets of Virginia City. It was on Billy Bay that Virginia made her famous, futile ride to save the life of her husband, Jack, hanged by the vigilantes in March 1864. It was one race he didn't win.

Lewis and Clark County Racetrack*

MONTANA made great contributions to the sport of horse racing in the United States, producing national champions. But the widespread popularity of the sport was due to early local enthusiasm. Nowhere in Montana was there a better demonstration than in the first territorial fairs. Beginning in 1868, Lewis and Clark County offered the first organized regional races and substantial purses. In 1870, the territory's first regulation track at the Lewis and Clark County Fairgrounds attracted participants from far distances. Although other cities, including Butte and Bozeman, later formed the Montana Circuit, the Helena track continued to be at the heart of the sport in Montana. Racetracks at Anaconda and Butte, today both victims of real estate development, brought Montana horse racing a national focus, but the Montana Circuit, later including Billings, Glendive, Missoula, and Great Falls, traces its origins directly to the first territorial fairs and the track at the Lewis and Clark County Fairgrounds. The racetrack is one of the oldest one-mile tracks west of the Mississippi, and it is Montana's only surviving racetrack from early territorial days. Although a new building has partially obliterated the track's east end, its remaining footprint is a precious and endangered landmark.

West Yellowstone

UNION PACIFIC RAILROAD officials began to build a branch line from Ashton, Idaho, to the western edge of Yellowstone Park in 1905. As workers laid the final tracks in 1907, the Forest Service platted the town of West Yellowstone. Private businesses prospered, serving tourists ferried back and forth to the park by stagecoach. West Yellowstone grew around the 1909 Union Pacific Depot.* Built of log and welded tuff—that's volcanic rock—gathered along the railway line, the depot's style foreshadows the Rustic architecture the National Park Service later adopted. In 1925, the Union Pacific hired Gilbert Stanley Underwood to design a dining lodge and employee housing at West Yellowstone. It's interesting that Underwood, the park's architect, was designing the world-renowned Ahwahnee Hotel at Yosemite National Park at the same time. It's no coincidence that the West Yellowstone dining lodge* looks much like the Yosemite hotel. Next time you visit West Yellowstone, take note of the depot and Underwood's dining lodge. The buildings represent early park tourism and the Rustic style.

Mackay Gallery of Russell Art

NEW JERSEY–BORN stockbroker Malcolm Mackay came to Red Lodge in 1899 on a hunting trip and fell in love with Montana. In 1901, he and partner Charlie Wright established the Rosebud Land and Cattle Company. Mackay continued to live in New Jersey but frequently brought his family to the Montana ranch. In 1911, Mackay met artist Charlie Russell in a New York gallery where Charlie's wife, Nancy, was peddling her husband's work. The Mackays welcomed the Russells into their home. Mackay was an astute collector of art and realized the artist's talent. Some of Russell's most famous paintings eventually hung in the Mackays' home in Tenafly, New Jersey. When Mackay died in 1932, his widow realized that the collection belonged in Montana, where many could enjoy it. So in the late 1940s, the family arranged for the new Northern Hotel in Billings to display their paintings. In 1952, despite public outcry, the prized Russell collection in Great Falls's Mint Bar—once Russell's favorite haunt—sold for $225,000 and went to Fort Worth, Texas. To keep the Mackay collection in Montana, the Montana Historical Society campaigned to purchase it for the family's asking price of a mere $50,000. The thirty-eight pieces included oil and watercolor paintings, sculptures, and sketches. Society director K. Ross Toole appealed to Montanans using every angle, including the recent shameful loss of the Mint Bar's Russell art. Donations came from cattle auctions, schools, rodeos, lotteries, and door-to-door canvassing. In December 1952, the collection moved from Billings to the newly opened Montana Historical Society museum on the state's capitol campus. In 1974, the enlarged gallery became the Mackay Gallery of Russell Art. The Mackay collection forms the core of one of the most important displays of Russell's work.

Rodeo

MONTANA cowboys say that rodeos weren't born, "they just growed" out of custom and necessity. And nowhere is there a richer rodeo heritage than where the Big Sky meets the rolling prairie. Cowboys honed their skills on long overland cattle drives to get livestock to market. But as the Northern Pacific steamed across America's last frontier in 1883, barbed wire encroached on the open range. Ranches needed fewer hands, and the cowboy life passed into legend. A genre emerged that employed cowboys when ranches did not. Wild West shows marketing cowboy skills as entertainment took the Old West across the country and abroad. At home in Montana, state and local fairs provided an outlet for homegrown cowboys and cowgirls to show off their considerable skills. After World War I, rodeo came into its own, taking its formal elements—the grand entry, clowns, and trick riding—from the disappearing Wild West shows. Fannie Sperry Steele and Marie Gibson, who performed in both early rodeos and Wild West–type entertainments, witnessed the transition as rodeo matured into a profession. The first national professional rodeo organization formed in 1929, bridging the final transition between the Old West and the modern era. The days of the range and cowboy gatherings after roundup might be gone, but the skills they perfected flourish across the West as sport and entertainment. Montana offers spectacular rodeos in every corner of the state in nearly every month of the year.

Vance Lodge*

✳ RUGGED outdoorsman and adventurer Andrew Vance came to Montana from Iowa in 1880. He guided buffalo hunters into the Yellowstone Valley to feed Northern Pacific Railroad crews and later guided Yellowstone Park visitors. He followed the gold rush to Alaska's Klondike and came back to Montana. In 1914, Andy, his wife, Ella, and daughters Maud and May homesteaded near the North Fork of the Flathead River. Andy worked on a trail crew in Glacier Park, ran a sawmill, and hunted and trapped for food while Ella kept an extensive garden. In 1920, Andy began to replace the family homestead with a two-story log lodge that accommodated his family and the guests Andy packed into the wilds of northern Montana and southern Canada. The remote, scattered North Fork community soon found a place for local gatherings at Vance Lodge. Andy died in 1924 when he was hit by a train near Belton, and Ella died in 1929, but their home remained at the heart of the community. Daughter May married the local postmaster, and the lodge served as post office during the 1930s. The lodge escaped the devastating 1988 forest fires and is still a seasonal home to the extended Vance family. It's a place of good luck and friendship to Andy's descendants.

State Song

✳ IN 1910, comedy star and composer Joseph E. Howard performed in Butte. The community warmly welcomed him, and after the performance, Mrs. E. Creighton Largey hosted a reception. Mrs. Largey joked that Howard had slighted Montana by including a song about Illinois in his production. Howard said that there were no songs about Montana. "So why don't you write one?" she asked. Taking up the challenge, Howard partnered with the only writer present, Charles Cohan, city editor of the *Butte Miner*. Half an hour later, they finished the composition. Before the evening's end, everyone had joined in singing the catchy refrain. "Montana" debuted the next day in Helena. The crowd demanded that Howard repeat it twelve times. Governor Edwin L. Norris was in the audience and later proposed "Montana" as the state song. The writers agreed, suggesting the proceeds go to charity. The Montana Children's Home (now Shodair Hospital) became the beneficiary. Even today, Shodair distributes the sheet music. Inspired by the state's hospitality, the song never brought its creators a penny, yet it has benefited Montana children and delighted us all.

Going-to-the-Sun Road*

Going-to-the-Sun Road, a National Historic Landmark, is a phenomenal work of civil engineering, completed in 1934. Built without bulldozers, motorized graders, and other modern equipment in virtually uncharted territory, this two-lane highway through Glacier National Park showcases glacial lakes, alpine tundra, and cedar forests. The name Going-to-the-Sun comes from a high mountain east of Logan Pass. The road skirts the base of Going-to-the-Sun Mountain. Several legends explain the mountain's unusual name. The Blackfeet say it translates, "To the Sun He Goes." According to one legend, Napi the Creator came to help when the people were in trouble. His work done, Napi returned to the sun, leaving his portrait on the rocky face of the mountain peak. Another legend says that Napi angered the people and fled to the highest mountain. There on the peak, he turned himself into a rock where he can still watch out for his people. Another story goes that in 1887 novelist James Willard Schultz and Blackfeet hunter Tail-Feathers-Coming-in-Sight-Over-the-Hill discussed the peak and agreed it was a good place for a vision quest. The two named it Going to the Sun. Whatever you believe, the name of the road that seems to wind ever skyward is fitting for a road-building milestone and masterpiece.

Feeding Thousands

✦ GLENN MONTGOMERY cooked for several of the crews that built Going-to-the-Sun Road* and was head cook for West Glacier Park. But never in his career did he feed more people than on July 15, 1933, the day Going-to-the-Sun Road was dedicated. Park officials expected to serve lunch to twenty-five hundred people before the opening ceremony. The day before, Montgomery gathered his groceries, including 500 pounds of red beans, 125 pounds of hamburger, 36 gallons of tomatoes, 100 pounds of onions, and 15 pounds of chili powder. The brew bubbled on four woodstoves in nine copper-bottomed washtubs until midnight. Crews transported the first batch of hot chili up to Logan Pass and transferred it to waiting cook fires to keep it hot. Meanwhile, back at headquarters, Montgomery prepared a second batch that cooked the rest of the night. Nineteen-year-old Ernest Johnson, who worked on the road's construction at forty cents an hour, stayed up all night helping to stir the chili. The morning dawned sunny and clear, drawing four thousand people to the festivities on Logan Pass. The chili stretched thin, but with additional hot dogs and coffee, everyone got something to eat. Johnson later said that he slept through the event but helped clean up the mess. He never saw so many paper plates in all his life.

Books

✦ EARLY Montana pioneer Granville Stuart tells a story that proves his insatiable love of reading. Granville and his brother James were among the first residents of the Deer Lodge Valley. In late winter 1861, word came to the Stuart brothers that a man by the name of Neil McArthur had left a trunk of books in the care of a Hudson's Bay trader in the Bitterroot Valley. The brothers were so starved for reading material they immediately packed dried meat and blankets, saddled their horses, and started the hazardous 150-mile trip to the Bitterroot Valley. It was nearing spring, and the Big Blackfoot, Hellgate, and Bitterroot rivers were very dangerous and difficult to cross. Once at their destination, the brothers feasted their eyes on the books, but the trader insisted that he had no authority to sell them. The Stuarts pleaded until finally he agreed to loan them five books at five dollars each. They promised to pay McArthur when he returned to claim them. The Stuarts could hardly make up their minds which books to choose. They finally settled on illustrated editions of Shakespeare and Byron, a French Bible, Adam Smith's *Wealth of Nations,* and Headley's *Napoleon and His Marshalls.* McArthur never returned to the Bitterroot Valley, but the Stuart brothers wore the books to tatters and never regretted the dangerous trip to obtain them.

Montana Club*

PRIVATE men's clubs had long been a fixture in cities back East, and as frontier settlements like Helena evolved from mining camps to towns, the uncouth image would no longer do. The first members of Helena's far-famed Montana Club set out to prove their town as cultured as any other with elegantly appointed rooms beautifully furnished for the cultured enjoyment of its 130 members. Rules were strict. There was no gambling on club premises, and no women were allowed except at special events. The reading room artistically displayed all the latest newspapers. Missing was the popular *Police Gazette* because it was printed on pink paper and considered tacky. Bylaws forbade loud talking, eating, or drinking in the library, and neither were dogs or sleeping on the sofas allowed. By the 1890s, rules relaxed and the club installed a basement bowling alley where, at certain times only, ladies were welcome. Another fund-raising scheme extended special ninety-day memberships to officers stationed at Fort Harrison. But some of the officers drank too much, became unruly, and even smuggled women into the club.

Times do change! In the 1940s, the Montana Club installed slot machines in its lounge and opened the bar to women.

Rex Bar*

A TWIST of fate landed sixteen-year-old German immigrant Alfred Heimer a job with Buffalo Bill Cody's Wild West Show in 1894. Although the irascible Colonel Cody fired young Heimer three times during that first day, the youth remained as steward of Cody's private railway car until 1903, developing a close friendship with the famous frontiersman. The genial Heimer then settled in Billings. He built the Rex Bar around 1909. It served such colorful patrons as his friends Buffalo Bill and Will James. Early advertisements extolled Heimer's German lunches and promised the "Best Beer in Town." In 1917, addition of the third floor converted Heimer's "nice furnished rooms" into a classy hotel that hosted many dignitaries, including the great Crow chief Plenty Coups, who stayed there in 1921 en route to Washington, D.C. Under new proprietors, the Rex flourished during Prohibition; the bar simply went under cover. The hotel closed in 1974 and narrowly escaped demolition. Award-winning rehabilitation has restored the Rex to its former glory, and the hospitality first offered by Alfred Heimer is again a Billings tradition.

Fort Peck Theatre*

WHEN President Franklin D. Roosevelt authorized the construction of the Fort Peck Dam in 1933, it created an "instant" town with a population of ten thousand. Residents needed social and recreational diversions in this remote area of Montana. The Army Corps of Engineers designed and constructed the Fort Peck Theatre in less than nine months at a cost of nearly ninety thousand dollars. The theater opened November 16, 1934, as a movie house.

Seating capacity was twelve hundred, and continuous showings ran twenty-four hours a day, seven days a week, during the construction of the Fort Peck Dam. Patrons sometimes braved lines as long as seven blocks to see the newest films for a forty-cent floor or thirty-cent balcony seat. The theater remained a movie house until 1968, and films are still sometimes shown with a modern 16 mm projector. The theater's original carbon-arc projectors, however, remain in operable condition. Built to resemble a Swiss chalet, its cut-out balustrades, false balconies, champhered beams, and herringbone-patterned siding are artistically unsurpassed in Works Progress Administration construction in Montana. The Fort Peck Theatre now houses a professional theater company and is a cultural treasure serving almost eight thousand theater-goers every summer.

Yucca Theatre*

An optimistic, cheerful nature and a keen sense of humor helped make Treasure County legislator David Manning instrumental in getting Montana "out of the mud." An engineer and contractor, Manning did much for Montana's rural communities, initiating improvements such as electricity, paved roads, dams, and irrigation systems in sparsely populated areas. Known for his clever solutions to difficult problems, Manning was fair and patient and often crossed political party lines when others could not. Upon his retirement, Manning had served in the Montana House and Senate from 1932 to 1985, longer than any other legislator in the nation. Just before he entered politics, Manning and his brother, Jim, designed and built the Yucca Theatre in Hysham. The landmark theater well represents the huge popularity of talking pictures. Typical of Manning's visionary intuition, its construction in 1931 raised community morale, ensuring the community of Hysham's survival during the Great Depression. Attached living quarters served as Manning's family home during his long political service. In 1992, the Manning heirs donated the facility to the Treasure County '89ers. It is now a fantastic museum.

Washoe Theatre*

SEATTLE-BASED theater architect B. Marcus Pinteca drew the plans for the two-hundred-thousand-dollar Washoe Theatre, which opened in 1936. The Washoe in Anaconda and Radio City Music Hall in New York were the last two American theaters built in the Nuevo Deco style, a lavish form popular for vaudeville theaters. From the street, the Washoe's brick exterior gives little indication of the breath-taking splendor that lies beyond the etched-glass doors. Designer Nat Smythe of Hollywood created the sumptuous interior, adorning the walls and ceilings with murals. Colors of cerulean blue, salmon, rose, beige, and yellow are enhanced by abundant copper plating, silver and gold leaf, and ornamental ironwork. Early advertisements extolled the fine "Mirrophonic Sound" system and the large auditorium that seated one thousand movie-goers. Admission for first-run films was thirty-five cents. Today, the Washoe is one of the nation's best-preserved theaters with original fixtures and equipment still in use. Although a ticket costs a little more than thirty-five cents, you can still catch a flick in this beautiful landmark.

Club Moderne*

IT was a grand and gala event in Anaconda on October 9, 1937, when John "Skinny" Francisco debuted his luxurious establishment to an eager public. Souvenir roses and etched liquor glasses commemorated the long-awaited occasion. The Club Moderne is today a premier example of the Art Deco style, especially noteworthy for its pristinely preserved interior. The style, introduced to America at a Paris exposition in 1925, was a completely new "modern" style, the ultimate architectural expression of the machine age. The club's gently rounded facade embellished with smooth Carrara glass panels elegantly emphasizes its streamlined proportions. Original neon lighting boldly illuminates the facade. Bozeman architect Fred Willson designed the building, which was constructed by Theodore Eck of Anaconda and finished entirely by local craftsmen. The henna and tan interior includes the original inlaid woods, leather panels, chromium and leather furniture, and Formica tables. Renowned as "the king of such places," the club attracts Art Deco enthusiasts from across the nation and beyond and has become a true icon for connoisseurs.

Science and Technology

Savenac Nursery*

WHEN the Forest Service celebrated its one hundredth anniversary, it recalled one historic site in Montana that played a major role in its history. Creation of the National Forest Service in 1905 brought Elers Koch, one of the nation's first professional foresters, to inspect and evaluate the Forest Reserves of Montana and Wyoming. As forest supervisor of the Bitterroot and Lolo National Forests in 1907, Koch happened upon the abandoned homestead of a German settler named Savannach in Mineral County. He thought it a perfect spot to establish a tree nursery. Work began in 1908. As the first pine seedlings were ready for transplant in 1910, fire swept through the region, burning 3 million acres of timber and destroying the nursery. The disaster made fire prevention and conservation a primary mission of the Forest Service. Reforestation figured prominently in that goal, and so the Forest Service wasted no time in rebuilding the nursery. Savenac became the largest tree nursery in the Northwest, producing up to 12 million trees annually. Regional reorganization closed the nursery in 1969, but during its long service, Savenac pioneered much of the theory and practice of silviculture right in Montana's Mineral County.

Telegraph Lines

BROTHERS John A. and Edward Creighton came west scouting the first transcontinental telegraph lines from Omaha, Nebraska, to the West Coast. Temporarily settling in Virginia City, Edward financed the first building made of locally quarried stone. The Creighton Stone Block* is one of Virginia City's most beautiful buildings, restored to its original appearance, with nine gracefully arched openings defining three separate storefronts. The building has special significance. In 1866, the Creightons, who had constructed the first transcontinental telegraph line in 1861, brought this critical link to Montana Territory. From a pole planted at the corner of the Creighton Block, Montana's first telegraph line connected to Salt Lake City. Edward Creighton died in 1874, and, following his wishes, his widow endowed Omaha's Creighton University, the first Catholic university in the United States. His brother, John Creighton, partnered with Butte's fourth Copper King, Patrick Largey, who, before he made his fortune, worked for the Creightons constructing telegraph lines. The State Savings Bank of Butte and the Speculator Mine were among their joint enterprises.

Time

THE British railroads established the first time zone in 1847, and American time zones were first proposed in 1868. As the tracks of the railroad crept across the United States, the need for standardized timekeeping became more critical. Scientists urged the railway industry to implement some kind of standard system so that trains could keep a schedule. As the Northern Pacific completed its run across Montana in 1883, the U.S. railroad industry implemented a "Standard Railway Time System" and established five time zones. As the clock ticked toward noon on Sunday, November 18, 1883, the clock at the railway depot in Helena's Sixth Ward advanced twenty-seven minutes and Helena adopted Mountain Time. Within a year, two hundred cities in the five different time zones across the United States had adopted Standard Time. In October 1884, at the behest of President Chester Arthur, forty-one delegates from twenty-five nations met in Washington, D.C., for the International Meridian Conference. Although all parties agreed on the necessity of international accord, that would not come until an act of Congress in 1918. The Standard Railway Time system remained the subject of much local controversy in Montana, but it kept the trains running on time.

Meriwether Lewis and a Forensic Mystery

THE Masonic Grand Lodge in Helena owns one of Montana's most mysterious and intriguing treasures. Meriwether Lewis's Masonic apron is not only a historically significant artifact but also a beautiful piece of artful handiwork. Hand-painted symbols and emblems significant to Masonry embellish the hand-sewn silk apron. In times past, members wore their aprons to reveal Masonic affiliation while traveling in dangerous situations. Meriwether Lewis certainly followed this practice on the expedition and was the first Mason to travel in Montana. Lewis was traveling along the dangerous Natchez Trace in Tennessee when he died of gunshot wounds under mysterious circumstances in 1809. Whether he committed suicide or was murdered remains in question. Family members believed that the apron was in his breast pocket when he died. The apron passed through several generations until 1924 when the Masons of Missouri purchased it from the widow of a distant Lewis relative. In 1960, Montana's retiring grand master, Joseph Hopper of Billings, bought the apron for five hundred dollars and gave it to the Grand Lodge Museum* in Helena. Several dark rust-colored stains mar the front. Samples of the stains tested at the University of Oregon revealed both deer and human blood, but only a sample of Lewis's DNA could determine if the human blood on the apron belonged to Lewis. How Lewis died is still debated, but during refurbishing of his tomb in 1928, an examination of his skull revealed a bullet hole in the back, unlikely evidence of suicide. A Tennessee coroner's jury in 1996 agreed evidence warranted exhumation of Lewis's remains. This would also open the door for further testing of the apron's human blood for DNA. But the National Park Service, caretaker of Lewis's grave and monument, has denied the request.

Hydroelectric Power at Thompson Falls

Missoula senator Edward Donlan, Dr. Everett Peek, and Arthur Preston organized the Thompson Falls Light and Power Company in 1910. Its purpose was to develop electricity for the community and to promote the concept of a hydroelectric power station. The monumental project promised progress and opportunity for the little frontier town along the riverbank. In anticipation, Dr. Peek built a hospital near the proposed power plant site. In 1911, the county erected two steel bridges across the Clark Fork River, retiring the old cable-drawn ferry. The Thompson Falls Power Company constructed a small plant to serve the community and the project itself. The town bustled, construction boomed, and a glorious future seemed inevitable. The newspaper confidently predicted lucrative future projects. By 1917, the plant supplied thirty thousand kilowatts of electricity to the region, crossing into Coeur d'Alene, Idaho. But after World War I, no more major projects boosted the local economy, and men like Senator Donlan and Dr. Peek, who initially championed those ideas, had already left town to find their dreams someplace else. The power company dismantled most of its buildings, leaving Thompson Falls to survive on its own. The surviving Hydroelectric Dam Historic District's* structures are an excellent example of early-twentieth-century hydroelectric technology.

Weather

✵ LEWIS and Clark made the first weather observations in Montana in 1805. In 1814, the U.S. Surgeon General ordered surgeons to keep weather diaries. The advent of telegraph operations in 1845 opened the possibilities of forecasting storms from place to place. According to the National Weather Service, in 1867 at Fort Shaw,* the army made the first informal weather observations in Montana since Lewis and Clark. Volunteers began regular weather observations in Deer Lodge in 1869 and in Virginia City in 1871. Other towns followed suit, but there was no formal organization. The government tapped the U.S. Army to begin what became the forerunner of the National Weather Service, called the Signal Service, in 1878. It was so-called because flags signaled the various conditions. In Montana, the army kept the first regular official records at Fort Keogh* near Miles City. The Signal Service began in Helena in September 1879. Equipment was installed on top of Parchen's drug store* at Main and Broadway. Several upstairs rooms held the barometer and weather office. There were seven daily observations; colored flags flown on the rooftop advised the community about weather conditions.

Telephones

✵ IN 1876, a decade after the first telegraph line linked Montana Territory to the States, Alexander Graham Bell uttered his famous words: "Watson, come here; I want you." If Bell had known how famous those words would become, he likely would have said something else into the first telephone. With those words, however, new technology changed the world. Telephones had Montana buzzing with a severe case of "telephonitis." Before there were commercial telephone exchanges and phones in homes, makeshift lines were rigged between telegraph offices in different towns. The *Helena Herald* reported that just before a severe thunderstorm, a Whitehall man stopped in the Helena telegraph office to see if he could talk with his wife, who was visiting friends in Troy. Finally getting her on the line, he refused to believe the voice was really that of his wife. He asked her to say or do something to convince him. Just then a tremendous streak of lightning jolted through the wires and knocked the man flat. As he regained his footing, he exclaimed, "That's the ole woman, sartin—only she's grode a l-e-e-tle more powerful sence she left home."

Refrigerators

MONTANA housewives read the newspapers and kept up with modern trends. They looked forward to modernizing their kitchens with the latest conveniences. One of the most important advances was home refrigerators, first introduced in 1911. In 1918, Kelvinator introduced the first refrigerator with an automatic control. The first freezer units were on the market in the 1920s, and in 1922 one model with a water-cooled compressor, two ice-cube trays, and nine cubic feet of space cost a whopping $714! Consumers had two hundred different models to choose from. These early electric models usually had a separate compressor driven by belts attached to motors installed in the basement or adjoining room. During the holiday season of 1930, the new Kelvinator refrigerator included the Kelvinator tray, making preparation of frozen desserts easy. Recipes for frozen delights were all the rage. Particularly popular were cranberry ice, frozen plum pudding, and a frozen Christmas salad made with cream cheese, green peppers, chopped pimiento, lemon juice, and whipped cream. Invention of the flexible ice-cube tray was still to come in 1932, and mass production of refrigerators didn't get started until after World War II.

Getting There Was Half the Battle

Camel Trains

✸ In the earliest days of the Montana mining camps, transportation was slow, and miners often waited in vain for ox-drawn freight wagons and mule trains to deliver supplies. Bad weather frequently delayed such essential items as mail, flour, and, of course, whiskey. Stories abound about freighters caught in winter storms. Such delays caused the rationing of supplies and brought on the infamous flour riots in Virginia City. Private companies tried to improve the delivery system, and some began to employ camel trains to carry goods over the Mullan Road to remote mining camps. It sounded like a great idea. Camels could carry up to one thousand pounds of flour each, they needed little food and water, and they plodded along at a slow but even pace. They were rather like today's postal service: neither rain nor sleet nor snow seemed to stop them. But there was one problem. Bullwhackers and muleskinners detested the ungainly critters and dreaded meeting them on the trail. A mule train could smell the peculiar odor of camel from a long way off. Camel stench on the wind made horses and mules impossible to control. A mule train laden with a supply of whiskey earmarked for the Fourth of July met a camel train on a narrow road, and the mules stampeded. When it was over, whiskey soaked the ground, the Fourth of July was dry, and the camel experiment was over.

Fort Benton and the Old Forts Trail

✹ THE American Fur Company established Fort Benton in 1846, naming it for U.S. senator Thomas Hart Benton, the company's congressional ally. As the gold rush began, a settlement outside the post walls grew. Steamboats brought prospectors, traders, settlers, and merchandise to this northwest gateway. In turn, they carried buffalo hides, gold bullion, and passengers back to the States. Fort Benton's merchant princes—I. G. Baker, T. C. Power, and the Conrad brothers—sent traders with rifles and whiskey into Canada to lure Indian peoples away from trade with the Hudson Bay Company. Resulting lawlessness brought the North West Mounted Police into present-day Alberta and Saskatchewan. As the Mounties worked to curtail the whiskey and gun trade, these same Fort Benton companies carried tons of food, mail, and treaty rations to Canada and returned with buffalo bones and hides, furs, wolf pelts, and coal. Until the railroad replaced steamboats in 1883, Fort Benton was the southernmost point and the most critical link in this international supply line. The Montana legislature has officially recognized the eastern branch of the route as the Old Forts Trail.

Mullan Road

✹ MULLAN PASS takes its name from John Mullan, who led an expedition through the area in 1853 and located the pass over the Continental Divide. In 1859, Mullan returned to present-day Montana to build a wagon road connecting Fort Benton, Montana Territory, with Walla Walla, Washington. Completed in 1860, it was the first engineered road in the territory, 624 miles long. Initially designed for military traffic, it never really served that purpose. After the gold rush began in 1862, primarily miners and freighters used the road, although in places it was too narrow for wagons. It never became a major thoroughfare. Portions of the road with its historic wagon ruts still exist in several locations in western Montana. Sections of the road near Alberton in Mineral County are especially well preserved. Mining traffic primarily used the stretch of the Mullan Road between Fort Benton and Helena. A portion of it runs over Mullan Pass. In September 1862, three Masons held the first lodge meeting in Montana on the pass. The Northern Pacific Railroad, with the help of Chinese workers experienced in blasting, built the Mullan Tunnel under the pass in 1883. The treacherous work required construction of a temporary switchback route over the pass to meet the September 1883 deadline for completion of the line at Gold Creek.

Old-time Billboard

ADVERTISING along roadways with signs and billboards is not a modern innovation. Indeed, along well-traveled roads in Montana and elsewhere, businesses sometimes took advantage of advertising to get the word out. For example, freighters, stages, light spring wagons, and lone horsemen traveling into Townsend in the late 1800s and early 1900s couldn't miss the bright advertising of a local business. Painted directly on a vertical limestone rock wall is a sign measuring 8 feet high by 15 feet long. The historic billboard is visible along the Indian Creek Road. The sign reads "The Best in Town, McCormick's Livery and Feed Stable, Near Depot—Townsend" in bright black and orange paint against the gray rock background. Ficklin T. McCormick came to Townsend and established the livery in 1883. Although he had some smaller competition, McCormick's was always the largest livery in town. With the advent of the automobile in 1915, McCormick sold his business, once an essential fixture in downtown Townsend. McCormick's Livery and Feed Stable sign* is one of several local examples of early advertising and a vivid reminder of the time when horses were the only mode of transportation.

Stage Travel

STAGECOACH travel was not very comfortable and was often unpleasant. If the weather was cold, tight-fitting clothing made for a miserable journey, and passengers sometimes found themselves seasick with the lurching motion. The best seat was always the one next to the driver, out in the open air. In 1866, the *Omaha Herald* published some tips for travelers that point out some of the discomforts of stage travel. For example, take small change to pay expenses, said the article. Some stage stop proprietors were notoriously bad tempered. The article goes on, "You should never shoot on the road as the noise might stampede the horses. If the team runs away, sit still and take your chances. If you jump out, nine out of ten times you will get hurt. Don't discuss politics or religion with fellow passengers, and don't swear or lop over neighbors when sleeping. If you have anything to drink in a bottle, pass it around. Don't point out where murders have been committed especially if there are women passengers. Don't keep the stage waiting, don't smoke a strong pipe inside the coach, and be sure to spit on the leeward side. At the stage stops, don't lag at the wash basin. Don't grease your hair because stage travel is dusty. And finally, don't imagine for a moment that you are going on a picnic. Expect annoyances, discomfort, and some hardship." After all these warnings, it's a wonder that anyone traveled at all.

Stage through the Canyon

FRANCES M. A. ROE wrote a lively account of a stage ride through the treacherous Prickly Pear Canyon in *Army Letters from an Officer's Wife.* Her account illustrates how creatively drivers dealt with terrible roads. Frances describes why she dreaded meeting an oncoming ox train on the very narrow, boulder-strewn road. Sure enough, they had not gone far when a huge freighter lumbered toward them. A sheer precipice dropped on one side and soared skyward on the other. It seemed a hopeless situation. The driver barked, "Get the lady out!" Men from the freighters sidled over. With no words spoken, they knew exactly what to do. They lifted the stage—trunks and all—up, over, and onto some of the boulders and led the horses between others. The horses stood at the edge of the precipice without a twitch while three teams of eight yokes of oxen passed by. "It made me ill," Frances wrote, "to see the poor patient oxen straining and pulling up the grade those huge wagons so heavily loaded. The crunching and groaning of the wagons, rattling of the enormous cable chains, and the creaking of the heavy yokes of the oxen were awful sounds, and above all came the yells of the drivers, and the sharp, pistol-like reports of the long whips." After the wagons passed, the men returned and matter-of-factly set the stage on the road. The process was repeated six or seven times as the stage traveled through the canyon.

Bridge to the Railroad

THE Dearborn River High Bridge*, built in 1897, spans the Dearborn River across a deep canyon eighteen miles south of Augusta. But the area has a longer history stretching back to generations of native peoples who used the crossing in their travels to seasonal hunting grounds. Although Lewis and Clark trekked through in 1805, the valley was in dangerous Blackfeet country and therefore remained pristine and unexplored by whites. Topographer P. M. Engel passed through in 1859 scouting the route for the Mullan Road. He described the timbered valley as very difficult to maneuver, cut up by sloughs and ditches. With the advent of the Montana Central Railroad in 1887, homesteaders began to settle the area and Augusta became the local trading center. The bridge is historically important because it provided critical access to the railroad for local residents, livestock, and goods. But it is also significant for its unique design. The deck attaches midway on the trusses instead of at the bottom or top. The King Bridge Company of Cleveland, Ohio, tailored the design for relatively light loads over the deep crossing. In 2002, Lewis and Clark County and the Montana Department of Transportation lifted the bridge off its abutments and set it down on the riverbank for repairs. Back in place and newly painted, this county landmark has a new lease on life.

First Trolleys

THE advent of the railroad and urban growth prompted a need for dependable intra-urban transportation. Between 1888 and 1890, there were twenty-seven attempts to establish street railway service in nine Montana cities, but credit goes to Billings for establishing the first operational system. Two bright yellow, horse-drawn cars ferried passengers in 1883. Business boomed temporarily when railway promoters offered twenty-five-cent tickets and coupons for free beer at a local brewery. But the company soon went out of business. Its two wayward horses refused to keep to a schedule. Montana first licensed automobiles in 1913, and gasoline engines, World War I, postwar inflation, and changing travel patterns took their toll on public transportation. The Billings Traction Company folded in 1917. Bozeman's system closed because of complaints that trolleys pushed aside snow, interfering with automobiles. Helena's last car entered the barn at midnight on New Year's Day in 1928; bus service began a few hours later. The Rainbow Hotel in Great Falls hosted a funeral in December 1931 for its trolleys. Guests filed past a battered streetcar and sang songs composed for the event, conceding that the trolleys "ain't gonna run no more." Missoula's streetcar service ended in 1932, Butte's ended in 1937, and Montana's last trolley bell clanged in 1951 with a final run between Anaconda's smelter and the town of Opportunity.

Airway Radio Station*

AVIATION captivated America during the 1920s, particularly when Charles Lindbergh flew solo across the Atlantic in 1927. The United States made rapid strides, and airfields opened all over the country. The town of Belgrade constructed Gallatin County's first airfield in 1929. Eight thousand people attended the opening of Siefert Field, causing the county's first traffic jam. By 1930, the United States had the world's most advanced airway system, and in 1935, Northwest Airways received federal approval to provide Montana with east–west airmail service. The U.S. Department of Commerce built one Airway Radio Station at Siefert Field. Federally constructed airway stations, two hundred miles apart along the airways, provided services critical to the development of civil aviation. The Siefert station housed the radio range and ground-to-air system used by airmail pilots on the Minneapolis to Seattle civil airway. Employees manned radio equipment twenty-four hours a day and gathered weather information, transmitting it over teletype. In the late 1930s, high-frequency VHF signals proved more reliable, and radio range equipment became obsolete. Gallatin County moved the station to nearby Pogreba Field in 1953. It's one of two such stations left in Montana and today serves as the Three Forks Airport terminal.

Billings Plane Crash

IT was two A.M. on Saturday, December 8, 1945, and a heavy curtain of falling snow made visibility nearly zero. Northwest Airlines pilot Captain George D. Miller and his copilot, First Officer Vernon W. Pfannkuck, fought to land their C-47 army transport plane at the Billings airport. The plane carried twenty-one overseas veterans, returning from recent combat duty. With the war in

Europe finally over, they were on the last leg of their journey, headed to Seattle for discharge or stateside reassignment. After two failed attempts at landing, the tower observed the plane turn to the south toward the rimrocks, a rocky escarpment that rises above downtown Billings. The landing lights disappeared into the snow. On the ground, roaring engines awakened neighbors asleep in their homes on Poly Drive. The pilot gunned the engines in a heroic final attempt to pull the nose up. A wing caught in the trees, and there was a muffled thud when the plane went down in the soft snow. Shooting flames cast an eerie orange glow in bedroom windows along Poly Drive. Ambulances and neighbors rushed the pilots and six other gravely injured survivors through the icy streets to the hospital. The *Billings Gazette* reported that rescue workers removed a dozen smoldering black and red charred forms, still in sitting positions, from the twisted metal. Billings had no facility to accommodate so many casualties, and victims were held near the depot in a warehouse while awaiting identification. Both the pilot and copilot died, but four lucky servicemen survived. The crash became a statistic, and few recalled the horror of that December night.

Law and Disorder

Vigilantes

★ VIGILANTES—acting outside the law—signed an oath of secrecy after the hanging of George Ives at Nevada City on December 21, 1863. They set to work, rounding up suspected road agents, including Bannack's Sheriff Henry Plummer, who they believed was the leader of the operation. Road agents had been terrorizing the countryside with murders and robberies in Beaverhead and Madison counties, making travel by stage, wagon, and horseback dangerous. Sheriff Plummer built the gallows on which he hanged Peter Heron in 1863. A year later on January 10, 1864, Plummer himself swung from the same gallows along with his two deputies, Buck Stinson and Ned Ray. Several vigilantes held the rope taut as Plummer sat on the shoulders of several others who dropped him. The men hoisted up Stinson and Ray. Ray continued to struggle, his hand in the noose against his neck. He finally strangled to death when vigilantes pulled his hand away from his throat. There are still heated debates among some Montana historians regarding Plummer's guilt or innocence. The contemporary accounts from a wide variety of people who were not involved with the vigilantes provide good reasons to believe that Plummer was guilty.

Virginia City Hanging

THE most spectacular of the extralegal vigilante hangings was a quintuple hanging on the roof beam of an unfinished building in Virginia City. On January 14, 1864, George Lane, Jack Gallagher, Frank Parrish, Haze Lyons, and Boone Helm died together in a small commercial building that still stands on Wallace Street. None of these men stood accused of murder, but rather each was found guilty of crimes associated with the robberies and other activities of the road agents. The five men were buried in the town cemetery, but because of the stigma surrounding them, residents established a second cemetery and most families removed the remains of their loved ones from "Boot Hill" to nearby Hillside Cemetery. The creation of Montana Territory on May 26, 1864, and the federal presence that Virginia City's designation as territorial capital in 1865 brought to Alder Gulch eventually ended the work of the original vigilantes. Their last hanging was that of Charles Wilson on September 25, 1867, on the outskirts of town for informing road agents about the cargo and schedules of Wells Fargo's stagecoaches. The original vigilantes of Beaverhead and Madison counties hanged at least thirty-one men. Other vigilante groups, however, continued to surface periodically during the later decades of the nineteenth century.

Virginia City Bank Robbery

WELL-KNOWN Madison County pioneer A. J. Bennett was the cashier at Henry Elling's bank in 1879 when a pair of desperadoes sauntered in one quiet afternoon. Bennett was behind the counter and asked what he could do for them. One reached into his vest and the other reached for his hip, and both drew revolvers, which they aimed at Bennett's head. One man produced a buckskin thong and tightly bound Bennett's hands behind him while the other pressed his revolver into Bennett's neck. Bennett had just unlocked the fireproof safe—bad timing—when the pair came in. One continued to press his gun into Bennett's neck while the other rummaged through the open safe. They gathered up about forty-five hundred dollars and told Bennett not to sound the alarm. They headed out to the street, and Bennett followed, crying "Murder! Robbers!" A third man was waiting with the horses. The three made off on the road to Yellowstone Park. In their haste, they dropped one of the revolvers. It was a cut-down Colt with the trigger removed. The robber who held the gun on Bennett had been holding the hammer back with his thumb; the slightest movement could have caused the gun to fire. It was a professional job. The robbers had stationed fresh horses every thirty miles all the way to Yellowstone Park. Yet they overlooked twenty thousand dollars in gold dust and seventy-five thousand dollars in currency. Authorities eventually apprehended the third man who held the horses. He claimed the other two gave him five hundred dollars and told him to get lost. He did ten years at Deer Lodge.* Years later, speculation still held that the two who got away were Frank and Jesse James. The Elling Bank* still stands on Wallace Street.

Execution Laws

SINCE early territorial days, Montana law dictated that executions be carried out in the county where the crime was committed. So in the first decades of the twentieth century, several counties built new jail facilities with permanent gallows. When Gallatin County built a new jail at Bozeman in 1911, it included one of these built-in gallows. In a small room with a high ceiling, a concrete staircase led up to a platform. A steel trap in the platform's floor gave way, allowing the condemned to fall free. These new gallows stood idle until the hanging of Seth Danner on July 18, 1924. According to tradition, the executioner was to remain anonymous. But to ensure his anonymity, two sets of ropes led from the gallows. Only one rope connected to the trap. Two men stood ready, each holding one of the ropes. At the signal, both men cut their ropes, but neither knew which of them had actually sprung the trap. The identity of the real executioner was unknown even to the executioners themselves. Laws concerning capital punishment changed very little during Montana's first century. However, in 1921, legislators amended the law concerning capital punishment for the first time since the creation of Montana Territory. Death by hanging was previously the only punishment allowed for murder in the first degree. Life in prison became an option. County jails and courthouses continued to serve as the required place of execution until 1983, when the legislature changed the law. Thereafter, executions have taken place at the Montana State Prison at Deer Lodge. The double-rope gallows in the former Gallatin County Jail* is still intact. The building now houses the Gallatin County Historical Society Pioneer Museum.

Darkest Chapter

THE largest gallows constructed in Montana was the death instrument for four men hanged simultaneously at Missoula on December 12, 1890. The four Indians executed at this hanging were the most men to die together in a legal execution in Montana. Sheriff William Houston of Missoula County obtained plans for the gallows from Cook County, Illinois, where authorities conducted a quadruple hanging in 1887. The Cook County sheriff also gave Sheriff Houston the four used ropes. All four men, convicted of murdering six white men, died on the huge trap-type gallows. Pierre Paul, Lala See, Antley, and Pascale admitted guilt in the three separate incidents, but they viewed their crimes as retaliation for whites killing Indians. White man's whiskey also played a role in some of the men's crimes. Their trials and executions form a chapter darker than most in the state's history of capital punishment for the shameful handling of the executions. Pomp and circumstance befitting a great civic event accompanied the somber occasion. The *Missoulian,* December 19, 1890, ran full-page headlines that set the tone for eight pages of details. The paper covered every aspect of each of the four hangings and offered racially charged comments. As was often the case, officials rebuilt the gallows to a smaller scale so that it could serve for one more hanging, that of John Burns at Missoula, two years later on December 16, 1892.

Sheriff Seth Bullock

From Montana's first legal hanging in 1875 to its last hanging in 1943, lawmen constructed a total of twenty-two gallows. Of these, six gallows served at hangings in more than one county, earning the epithet "galloping gallows." Legendary lawman Seth Bullock, who was sheriff of Lewis and Clark County before he moved on to Deadwood, South Dakota, built the first of Montana's galloping gallows for the execution of William Wheatley. The case involved the grisly murder of Austrian-born Franz Warl. Authorities discovered his mutilated corpse, hands tied behind him and the cord wrapped around his neck. Wheatley's hanging, pointedly scheduled for Friday the 13th of August, presented some logistical problems. The scaffold was quite high, and Sheriff Bullock realized he could not carry out the letter of the law, which prohibited uninvited citizens from witnessing hangings. He built a tall fence around the scaffold, but buildings crowded around courthouse square, and it was impossible to enforce privacy. So Sheriff Bullock changed the time specified in the death warrant from midday to midnight. Even with the change in time, a thousand spectators crowded on the surrounding rooftops to witness the hanging by the light of the moon.

3-7-77

THE meaning of the vigilante ultimatum, 3-7-77, has confounded historians. Does it define the dimensions of a grave or the time allowed to get out of town? Author Frederick Allen in *A Decent and Orderly Lynching* suggests that its first use was not until 1879 in Helena following the unsolved murder of John Denn. He suggests that the warning gives the time the stage left for Butte. But no theory is entirely logical. The fraternal organization of Masons offers the best explanation. Many of Montana's first pioneers were Masons, and the numbers may thus symbolize three events important to Masonry in Montana. They believe the 3 represents the three Masons present at the first lodge meeting atop Mullan Pass in 1862. The 77 symbolizes the Masons present at the first Masonic funeral at Bannack. Seventy-six Masons attended; the deceased, William Bell, was the seventy-seventh. The 7 is more elusive. It may represent the seven Masons who were among the twelve men who helped organize the vigilantes, or the seven Masons who planned Bell's funeral, or some think it represents the seven liberal arts. Only one thing is certain: the authors of 3-7-77 did their job well to keep it secret; its true meaning is one of Montana's most enduring mysteries.

Murder of Celestia Alice Earp

IN 1965 in the basement of a historic Main Street Bozeman building, workers discovered a tombstone embedded in the floor. The epitaph memorialized Celestia Alice Earp, who died in 1881. Historian Merrill Burlingame took up the mystery and discovered that Mrs. Earp, a Civil War widow from Ohio, had been the victim of a horrible crime. She was attempting to flee the territory with a spurned suitor in hot pursuit. As she boarded the stage from Red Bluff to Virginia City, the driver invited her to sit next to him atop the stage. This was considered the best seat, but it was not a good choice for Mrs. Earp. As she rode out in the open, John Douglass, the suitor, caught up with the stage near Sterling and pumped five bullets into her. Mrs. Earp died after painfully lingering for several days. Douglass stood trial. Convicted of murder, officials carried out his hanging in the yard of the Madison County Courthouse* in May 1881. There is no record of Mrs. Earp's burial, but Bozeman newspaper accounts say she requested that her remains be sent back to Ohio for burial. The building whose basement hid the tombstone for more than eighty years was not built until 1888. At the time of the murder, William Nevitt's hardware store on Main Street might have been the outlet for a grieving relative to order an engraved tombstone. Montana had no local tombstone makers until the mid-1880s. Perhaps Mrs. Earp's sister ordered the marker and for unknown reasons failed to pick it up. Nevitt's hardware burned, and somehow the tombstone ended up in the basement of the replacement Nevitt Block* at 107 Main Street, later the AMC Sullivan Photo Shop. Whatever the answer to this mystery, there is another equally curious. The tombstone, long displayed at the Caroline McGill Museum—the forerunner of the Museum of the Rockies—has subsequently disappeared.

Hangman's Tree

A LONE Ponderosa pine, just west of present-day Blake Street between Highland and Hillsdale, served as Helena's Hangman's Tree. It was the only tree left standing in 1865 after miners had denuded the countryside for cabins and sluices. Mary Sheehan Ronan attended school up the hill in a simple cabin at Rodney and Broadway. From the schoolyard, the children had a clear view of the lone Ponderosa. One morning as they arrived at school, the children saw the limp form of a man dangling from the tree. The boys ran up and down the gulch, speculating about the "bad man" who received such awful punishment. Mary later wrote: "I hated the talk. It made me shiver . . . that dreadful, pitiful object, with bruised head, disarrayed vest and trousers, with boots so stiff, so worn, so wrinkled, so strangely the most poignant of all the gruesome details. I tried to forget, but I have never forgotten." At least eleven men suffered this fate on the famed Hangman's Tree. The last of the eleven hangings took place in 1870 when vigilantes hanged Arthur Compton and Joe Wilson for the attempted murder of a local rancher. Photographer Mary Ann Eckert captured the grisly scene in a graphic, horrific photograph. Until recently, a copy of it graced the hallway of a Helena elementary school, a strong message that crime doesn't pay. In 1875, thousands thronged the neighborhood to cut a souvenir sliver from the tree when Reverend Shippen, a Methodist minister, cut it down. It was so dead and dry that he feared it would fall on his barn and kill his horse.

Patrick Largey's Murder

PATRICK LARGEY, Butte's fourth Copper King, was president of the State Savings Bank, located on the site of the present Metals Bank Building. In January 1898, miner Thomas Riley gunned Largey down as he sat at his desk. The shooting took place nearly three years to the day after the great powder explosion in the warehouses of the Kenyon Connell and Butte Hardware companies. Illegally stored dynamite caused the blast that killed at least fifty-nine and injured one hundred others. Riley lost a leg in the blast and held Largey personally responsible. Though Largey owned stock in the hardware business, he had no part in the disaster. But Riley, who could no longer work, demanded compensation. Largey and Riley had several violent quarrels, and the last culminated in Largey's murder. Charged, convicted, and sentenced to life in prison, Riley went to the federal prison at Deer Lodge* in 1898. He kept his union membership in Local No. 1. In 1910, 170 members signed a petition asking the governor and the Board of Pardons to review Riley's case.

But the influential Largey family made sure that nothing came of it. Riley wrote letters to friends, lawyers, priests, and legislators to no avail. After he had spent forty years in prison, he met Governor Roy Ayers during an inspection. Ayers found no bitterness left in him and granted the seventy-year-old a full pardon. Riley left Deer Lodge in 1937. He died in 1938 after little more than a year of freedom.

The Bishop of All Outdoors

REVEREND LEONARD CHRISTLER came west to Montana to do Episcopal missionary work along the High Line. The reverend helped build churches in Malta, Glasgow, and Havre. In his travels among the far-flung High Line communities, Christler styled himself the "Bishop of All Outdoors." Wearing a long black coat and broad-brimmed western hat, he used his gift of oratory to preach to the railroaders and homesteaders who hung on his every word. He was an enigmatic, magnetic figure. When the Christlers' friends, Judge Frank Carleton and his pretty wife, Margaret, decided to separate in 1921, rumors began to fly. Longtime Havre resident Louise Wigmore recalled, seventy-five years after the fact, that all the teenagers in Havre closely followed the romance between the minister and the judge's wife. In the fall of 1922, Havre police answered Mrs. Christler's call for help. Arriving at the Christlers' home, authorities found the reverend crumpled dead in the bedroom doorway and Margaret, shot through the heart, lying near him. The murder weapon lay near her. The coroner ruled the deaths murder-suicide—with Margaret pulling the trigger. And so Christler's widow, above any suspicion, took the train back to New York with her hand on her husband's coffin. But questions remained. Could Margaret, weakened by sleeping powder she had taken, have pulled the trigger of the heavy revolver not just once, but twice? Further, the diamond rings missing from Margaret's finger never surfaced. Anna Christler lived out her life, a quiet figure dressed in black. It seems fairly clear where the blame should lie, but we will never know for sure.

Lucy Cornforth

THE Montana State Prison at Deer Lodge* incarcerated women within its walls from territorial days until 1959. Some cases suggest that women may not have always received equitable treatment in Montana's all-male courtrooms. It was not until 1939, in fact, that female legislators crafted a bill changing the definition of jury from a "body of men" to a "body of persons," finally obligating women to serve as jurors. Lucy Cornforth of Miles City is one example of justice gone awry. In 1929, Cornforth was a single parent depressed over difficulties with a neighbor. Contemplating suicide, Cornforth purchased strychnine, poured it in a cup, and told her eight-year-old daughter what she intended to do. But Cornforth changed her mind and set the cup aside. The child, knowing what was in it, seized the cup, drank the poison, and died minutes later. Cornforth, charged with first degree murder, pled guilty. Her attorney argued that she was "intellectually deficient," and the judge sentenced her to life in prison. Cornforth was a model prisoner. After fifteen years, the warden wanted to approve her parole, and a sponsor agreed to employ her in his home. The judge who sentenced her refused, maintaining that Cornforth posed a threat to others. In 1954, a retired teacher asked the parole board to review Cornforth's case, but the board wrote, "She would not be able to cope on the outside. She only has the mentality of a twelve-year-old." No one else spoke on Cornforth's behalf, and she died in prison, fulfilling her life sentence. Likely Cornforth would have had a better chance in today's legal system.

Memorable Holidays and Traditions

Mining Camp Thanksgiving

✺ ABRAHAM LINCOLN set a precedent during his presidency proclaiming the national observance of Thanksgiving the last Thursday in November. In 1863, Harriet and Wilbur Sanders, the latter the soon-to-be-famous vigilante prosecutor, spent their first Montana Thanksgiving at Bannack. Goods were scarce, freight was slow arriving, and no one even thought about serving a turkey. Near neighbors invited Harriet and Wilbur along with Henry Edgerton, Wilbur's uncle, to Thanksgiving dinner. This neighbor wanted to make a good impression on the family. Edgerton was the newly appointed chief justice of the Supreme Court of Idaho Territory, which then included present-day Montana. Their host offered the invitation well in advance. He miraculously procured a turkey—an unheard-of, unbelievable luxury—for thirty dollars in gold dust, and paid a fortune to have it freighted all the way from Salt Lake City. Harriet wrote later that their Thanksgiving meal was as fine and beautifully cooked as any meal she ever enjoyed in New York City's finest restaurant. Unfortunately, their host failed to make a good impression. In early January, just weeks later, Sanders and the vigilantes saw to the hanging of Sheriff Henry Plummer, the same man who had hosted their Thanksgiving Day feast.

Thanksgiving in December

✴ THE first official observance of Thanksgiving after the creation of Montana Territory came in 1865. Although President Lincoln had established the last Thursday of November as Thanksgiving Day, following Lincoln's assassination President Andrew Johnson chose December 7 as the day of official observance. Residents of the mining camps paused in their relentless search for golden treasure and gave thanks for their good luck and for the end of the Civil War. Virginia City businesses closed. There were private celebrations and culinary preparations in many homes and restaurants. The *Montana Post* reported that sleighs were gliding merrily around town all day, men hobnobbed at the bars, and there was a singing party in the governor's office. The next year, 1866, at Last Chance, celebrations were more community oriented. Young ladies put on their pretties and attended the Firemen's Ball on Thanksgiving Eve at the Young America Hall. Markets were well supplied for Thanksgiving Day feasts. Shoppers could choose elk, deer, bear, sage hens, grouse, and pheasant. There was no mention of turkeys, however, at Thanksgiving tables on that particular holiday.

Thanksgiving Turkeys

✴ EARTHQUAKES rocked the Helena Valley in 1935 leaving significant damage in the Sixth Ward, especially along Railroad Avenue. In that neighborhood, a small commercial district* had grown to serve the Northern Pacific Railroad. One grocer lost more than his building. For years he had offered fresh-dressed turkeys as a specialty. No one questioned why the giblets of his birds never included gizzards. But the shopkeeper had a secret. His turkeys arrived via the Northern Pacific from an area that had once been extensively placer mined; the turkeys pecked around in the tailings. When he butchered the turkeys, he found that the stones collected in their gizzards were often not just pebbles, but gold nuggets. The grocer kept them in a huge jug hidden in his basement. Over the years, his stash of nuggets had grown so that the jug was almost full. When the earthquake struck, his building collapsed, burying the valuable treasure forever. Neighbor kids talked about the Sixth Ward's buried treasure for years, and it is buried there to this day.

Holiday Candy

HOLIDAYS often center around food, and that was just as true in times past as it is today. Children then, as now, begged for sweets, and mothers worried about their children eating too much candy. During the holiday season of 1876, the Bozeman newspaper reminded mothers that the best candy for children is that made at home. A recipe offered a more healthful alternative to store-bought sweets. The recipe said to take a coffee cupful of white sugar, add two tablespoons of water to dissolve it, and boil it in a bright tin pan until the liquid will crisp in water. Add a teaspoon vanilla, peppermint, or lemon flavoring and a quarter teaspoon cream of tartar. Pour the mixture into a buttered pan until cool enough to handle; then pull it like molasses candy until it is perfectly white. Lay it on a marble slab, cut it into mouthfuls, and lay on buttered paper. When children want candy, said the newspaper, by all means let them have this. And then they will not eat plaster of paris, chalk, starch, and poisonous compounds that will damage their stomachs and ruin their teeth. This just goes to show that mothers even back then worried about additives.

Logging Camp Christmas

LOGGING camps sprang up in western Montana in the late nineteenth century to support a huge demand for timber to fuel Montana's mines and smelters. Lumberjacks from Ireland,

Germany, Sweden, France, and many other places made the camps international melting pots. In 1899, a reporter for the *Anaconda Standard* wrote a wonderful description of Christmas in the logging camps. He wrote that a cast-off circular saw hung outside the door of every camp cookhouse. When dinner was ready, the cook banged the saw. Deep in the snow-covered forest, the cadence of the cook's call to dinner was sweet music to the hungry men. Lumberjacks had no day off, no Christmas tree among all the green pine trees they cut. But when the cook's call came on Christmas Day, the loggers came in at a faster pace than usual, for they had been anticipating this meal for weeks. The cook placed bowls of mashed potatoes and cranberries on the long tables. The men came in merry, red with cold. When all were seated, the cook would bring in the turkeys, big and brown and fragrant. As the savory smell wafted from the national bird, the feast began. This goes to show that the holiday spirit works its way into even the most remote places. May your holiday meal be just as wonderful as the loggers' feasts of yesteryear.

Santa

PARENTS today delight in their children's wonder at a visit from Santa. A century ago, parents were not so different. An article in the *Butte Miner* during the holiday season of 1899 discusses the tradition, practiced by some families, of hiding gifts on Christmas morning and leaving clues. One Butte family went to creative lengths to disguise their children's presents. One year, the parents chose an apple barrel in the cellar. In it they hid a typewriter and other items, covering the gifts with a top layer of apples. Another year the parents lifted their slumbering child from his bed, hid gifts in the mattress, and put him back before he so much as turned over. The best hiding place, however, was one in plain sight. The parents constructed a makeshift shelf that they installed beneath the dining room table. Upon Christmas morning, after searching in vain for evidence of Santa's visit, and despite the hints Santa left in a letter on the mantel, the children sat at breakfast hopelessly discouraged, not dreaming that the gifts were literally under their plates!

Missed Christmas

MRS. FRANCES BARTON won the *Glasgow Courier*'s Christmas Memory Contest in 1959 for a story about her family's missed Christmas. In 1924, Frances, her husband, and their six-month-old son lived in a two-room tarpaper homestead shack in northern Valley County near the Canadian border. Since early December, bad weather had kept the Bartons from making the fourteen-mile trip to the little general store and post office at Genevieve. Their reading material was worn out, their food supplies were dwindling, and they had had no mail or contact with the outside world for weeks. The Bartons hoped the weather would permit their team to get through, but Christmas morning dawned without the opportunity. They had a poor Christmas meal, sang a few hymns, and wished each other Merry Christmas, but it was a day like any other. Finally, two weeks into the new year, 1925, the weather broke, and a January thaw came to the homestead. On a sunny morning, Frances's husband made the trip to Genevieve. He returned with a month's worth of letters, cards, gifts, magazines, newspapers, and supplies. "Christmas finally came to the Barton family," Frances wrote, "and once again we felt in touch with the outside world."

Christmas Epidemic

AT Christmastime in 1885, a diphtheria epidemic should have kept all citizens in their homes behind closed doors. But contagion was little understood. Even Dr. Ben Brooke was powerless to protect his two small daughters. When one young daughter came down with the disease, he sent his five-year-old to friends on

Helena's west side, hoping she could avoid contagion. But it was too late, and both children died. An editorial in the *Helena Herald* asked if diphtheria was present in the Brooke household, why didn't Dr. Brooke quarantine his own family? Dr. Maria Dean, then chairperson of the Board of Health, responded that certain unnamed citizens had unlawfully removed quarantine flags she had placed on certain households. A few days later, the paper carried the death notices for Norma and Felix Kuehn and their nurse Mary Dunphy—all of whom died of diphtheria. Right next to these somber notices was an invitation to a church Christmas party for children of all ages. The announcement ended: "Let the church be crowded." When it came to convincing citizens of the dangers of contagion, the public was not so easy to educate.

A Halloween to Remember

ALICIA "LETTIE" CONRAD never let adversity get the better of her. Kalispell's beautiful Conrad Mansion* is now a museum, but back in October 1910, Lettie nearly lost her home to a disastrous fire. The entire town turned out to fight the blaze. Despite scorched walls and water damage, the house and its contents survived. Lettie devised a way to thank those who helped fight the fire. She planned a spectacular Halloween party and invited the entire town. Soggy fallen plaster, piled furniture, and a gaping hole in the roof became the setting for Dante's Inferno. Five hundred guests made their way to "hell" in the basement by way of a circular stairway built in the elevator shaft. Clammy wet canvas hung over the doorways; strings hung down along the dark path like cobwebs. On the first floor, Spanish moss dripped over the balcony and on the chandeliers. Dozens of lifelike cardboard and silk bats hung on invisible silken thread; fans kept the bats flying. The second story was purgatory, where a mass of wet, slick plaster covered the floors and mounds of it shaped like volcanoes covered the soggy beds. Special lighting simulating flames shot out of the craters. The third floor was paradise. Piled-up furniture covered in fresh flowers served as pathways; their sweet scent covered the acrid smell of smoke. After the tour, the guests gathered in the great hall. Just before the orchestra tuned up for the dancing, Lettie thanked all those who had helped save her home. The dancing commenced, and there was food and music until dawn. There will never be another Halloween party like it.

Index

Note: page numbers of entry titles appear in italics.

Bozeman, 5–6, 36, 64, 85, 180,
   185–86, 188
Bozeman Hotel, *36*
Bozeman, John, 36, 135
Bozeman Trail, 48, 79, 135
Bridge to the Railroad, *179–80*
Broadwater, Charles, 40, 105
Brooke, Dr. Ben, *197–98*
Brother Van, *126–27*
B Street Brothels, *110–11*
Bullock, Sheriff Seth, *187*
Butler, May, *74–75*
Butte, 52, 72–73, 82, 83, 85, 88, 112,
   118, 146–47, 154–55, 161–62, 180,
   190–91
Butte Explosion, *88–89*
Butte Speakeasy, *112*
Byrnes, Mollie, 98

Camels in Montana, *2*
Camel Trains, *175*
Cameron, Evelyn, *67–68*
Campbell, J. L., 92
Camp Disappointment, *31*
Cannon, C. W., 98
Canton Church, *131–32*
Capitol Dome, *95–96*
Capitol Hill, *95*
Carey, Nicholas and Mary, 47
Carroll, Bishop John B., *129–30*
Carroll College, 47, 95, 129, 143, 154
Cascade, 69
Castner, John and Mattie, 51–52
Cattle Dog, *5–6*
Centerville Ghost, *154–55*
Challenge at Elkhorn, *118–19*
Charley's Boot, *79–80*
Chicago Joe, *71–72*

Chinook, 84
Chippewa Indians, 59
Christler, Reverend Leonard, 191
Christmas Epidemic, *197–98*
Cinnabar, *86*
Clarke, Malcolm, 106, 157
Clark's Lookout, *27*
Clark, William A., *54,* 93, 97, 152
Clark, Captain William, 23, 25, 26,
   28, 29, 30, 31, 32
Club Moderne, *167–68*
Cohan, Charles, 161–62
Columbian Exposition, *92*
Comanche, *8–9*
Connor, Matt, 151–52
Conrad, Alicia "Lettie," 198–99
Content, Solomon, 83–84
Cooper, Gary, 69, 108
Copper King Mansion, *152*
Cornforth, Lucy, *192*
Crail Ranch, *103–104*
Crow Indians, 14, 16–17
Cruse, Thomas, 129–30, 132
Custer, General George, 19, 135–36
Custer's Heart, *19*

Dalton Memorial, *79*
Daly, Marcus, 9, 52, 97, 113, 120
Daly's Horses, *9*
Daniels County Courthouse, *112–13*
Darkest Chapter, *186–87*
Dean, Maria, *119–20*
DeBorgia Schoolhouse, *115–16*
Deer Lodge, 13, 77, 101, 107, 108, 173
Deer Lodge Prison, 150, 185, 186,
   190–91, 192
Deer Lodge Woman's Club, *107*
DeSmet, Pierre Jean, 13, 125